Super Doesn't Require a Cape

Clean laughs and steady lessons for real life

James Alexander

This is a work of humorous nonfiction/memoir-style storytelling. Certain names, identifying details, and events may have been changed or composite-created to protect privacy. Any resemblance to actual persons, living or dead, is coincidental.

First edition: 2026
ISBN: 979-8-218-93067-7

Table of Contents

CHAPTER 1
Cornfield Rules

Growing up in the Midwest, I have learned a lot about life.

Over the years, reflecting back, I learned a lot about myself and others too.

I still have much to learn, but the basics were developed in a small town.

In our neighborhood, trash day wasn't just trash day. It was a weekly personality check.

Everyone pretended they didn't care. In reality, everyone cared.

There was a correct time to roll out your trash can: the night before, after dinner, late enough to look normal, early enough to look responsible. If you put it out too early, you would look anxious. Like you'd been thinking about that garbage can since breakfast. Planning for it, waiting for it.

If you put it out too late, you looked like the kind of person who says, "I'll get to it when I get to it," and then wakes up to the sound of the truck leaving your dreams behind along with your cans in the garage.

The moment everyone heard someone's trash can rolling in the distance, the whole street turned into prairie dogs. Scurrying to get their collection to the finish line.

"Oh, ok" you'd think, peeking through the blinds. "They're doing it."

Then you'd do it too—but casually, not rushed. Like you were already going outside for something else. Like you had a business reason to be near your trash can.

You'd roll it to the curb and look around with an unconcerned expression, "Nice day today".

And if your neighbor was also out there, you'd exchange the Midwest greetings, small enough to avoid conversation, clear enough to count as decency.

"Hey there Bill" you'd say in silence.

"I see you Bob" he'd say in the same language.

"We're not going to talk about this" you'd think.

"Nope, not a word" he'd retort.

People say the Midwest is quiet. That's true—but it's not because we have nothing to say, we're just too busy getting things done.

In my hometown, bragging was allowed only in emergencies. If you talked big, somebody would stare at you like you had spinach in your teeth. Then they'd change the subject to the weather, which is the Midwest way of saying, "*We are not doing this today.*"

And the weather really could be a whole conversation in itself. It wasn't small talk. It was survival planning.

"Looks like snow," a man would say, standing outside in a coat that had seen better years.

"Yep," another man would reply, like he personally knew the clouds.

Then both of them would stare into the distance for a full minute, as if the sky might confess its intentions to them.

That's what I grew up in: quiet, practical, honest. Sometimes funny on accident. Sometimes funny on purpose, but never loud about it.

If you've never lived in the Midwest, you might picture cornfields, tractors, and people saying "ope" a lot. That's accurate. But there's another thing too—a steady kind of goodness.

The Midwest has an unspoken belief that character matters more than charisma. You don't win people with speeches. You win them with follow-through. You win them by returning a borrowed tool without losing the one tiny socket that makes the whole set feel incomplete forever.

When you're a kid, you don't label it. You just breathe it. It becomes your normal.

We had rules that were never written down: respect your parents, don't waste, don't act better than people. If you made a mess, you cleaned it. If you made a mistake, you owned it. If you borrowed something, you returned it clean—sometimes cleaner than you got it.

None of it was dramatic. Nobody was giving inspirational talks with music playing in the background. The lessons showed up like chores, like common sense, like the same gentle correction repeated until you finally got it.

And I mean repeated.

My parents were patient most of the time, but they were never uncertain. If I had done something wrong, it was addressed quickly, thoroughly but with loyal love. There was no movie-scene yelling. There was no long courtroom debate. Not that there was not discussions. We had them like all families, some stronger than others, but our parents were the parents, raising their children with the same values my grandparents had passed down—each of them simply trying to improve on what they were given. Difficulties were addressed with the same overall goal:

"That wasn't right. Let's fix it."

In our house, punishment was simple. No speeches. No negotiations. You just got grounded—and then you got assigned to the garden. Two hours in the tomato patch can do a lot for a young person's character, especially if that young person is thinking about a football game happening somewhere else without him.

I learned early that consequences can be calm. They don't have to be scary to be effective.

My dad left for work early. I mean early-early like "the birds are still asleep" early. He'd step out into the dark, start up a tired old car, and drive off like it was normal to be responsible before sunrise.

He never made a big deal out of it.

That's what made it a big deal.

I would go with him sometimes, along with my brother. Honestly, we were always agreeable because we knew there may be a caramel pecan roll from the local bakery in the deal.

Sometimes yes, sometimes no. We usually came out even though.

Even when we did not go with him, he would get home in time to wake us his own special way.

"*Daylights in the swamp*" or "*daylight is burning, you going to die in bed.*"

Dad didn't talk about work ethic. He just had it. He didn't talk about being a good father. He just was. He fixed what needed fixing. He kept the wheels on our life.

My mom kept the house running. She did it with a steady that seemed to be easy, which is how you know it wasn't easy. She carried a whole household with sure hands and a sure heart even with five young ones in tow.

My mom had a way of doing ten things at once without making you feel like you were a burden. She could cook, clean, listen, and solve a problem, all while making you feel like you mattered.

That isn't a small skill.

That's leadership.

If you have a mom like that, you already know: the real hero in your childhood didn't have a cape.

She had a grocery list and a laundry basket.

I grew up watching quiet heroes. People who didn't post about it. People who didn't announce it. People who would actually feel awkward if you called them heroes.

They'd correct you and say, "Nah. I just did what I was supposed to do."

That sentence right there is the Midwest.

Our neighborhood was full of quiet help. If someone's car wouldn't start, you didn't post about it. You walked over and brought jumper cables. After connecting them you would say, "Try it now."

When it started, you nodded like you personally knew electricity and had just convinced it to cooperate with you.

In wintertime, the neighborhood had its own system too. If you were the first one awake after a snow, you shoveled. Not just your own driveway. Sometimes you did your neighbor's sidewalk too. Not as a statement. Just because you could—and because you knew they'd do the same for you.

That's the kind of place that builds character.

And it builds that character in a sneaky way.

Because you don't realize you're being shaped until you leave.

Then you go somewhere else and notice little differences. You notice how some people talk like they're selling themselves. You notice how quickly people quit when something is inconvenient. You notice how often folks treat truth like it's optional.

And you think, *Oh. Back home, that was doing something good. I just didn't know what to call it then.*

Being super is holding down a steady home, learning from calm consequences, quiet help, and being cared for by adults who do the right thing so consistently that kids start to think it's normal.

Super doesn't require a cape.

CHAPTER 2
The Code of the Wave

If the Midwest had commandments, they wouldn't be carved in a stone. They'd be taped to the fridge in someone's handwriting.

"Cleanup after yourself."

"There is no trash fairy, take the garbage out."

"Pick up the kids...again."

"If you don't like dinner, tell us what you're making."

But there is another part of the Midwest that people don't mention as much.

It's not just quiet.

It's careful.

We don't waste words because words mean something. If you say you'll do something, you do it. If you promise to do it, you deliver. If you can't, you explain. You don't just evaporate like a bad Wi-Fi signal.

Growing up around that wires you a certain way.

You start to feel itchy when you're late. Guilty when you forget something small. You can be sitting in a perfectly good restaurant and suddenly remember you didn't return a phone call—now your food tastes different, because your conscience has pulled up a chair and wants to discuss it.

That's the Midwest. Built-in responsibility.

Sometimes it's a gift.

Sometimes it's a rash.

But I'd rather have that than the alternative. Because a person with no sense of responsibility is hard to trust—and trust is the whole point of community.

One funny thing about truly solid Midwestern people is that they don't know they're solid.

They'll say, "I'm just a regular guy," while quietly being the kind of guy who holds a whole family together.

Compliment them and watch the escape attempt.

You say, "Hey, you did a really good job."

They'll shift their weight like you just offered them a microphone on a karaoke stage at a fancy Japanese restaurant.

They will get uncomfortable for a moment and say, "Just doing what I'm supposed to do."

Or the classic: "It is what it is."

Or they may simply say, "Oh... yeah... I mean... it was nothing."

Nothing?

My friend, you just rebuilt my entire deck.

Sometimes I want to grab people by the shoulders and say, "Bud. You can just say 'thank you.' You won't burst into flames. The corn won't judge you."

Midwest is simple like that.

And then there's the "don't waste" rule, which was basically part of every small-town code of ethics.

We didn't waste food.

We didn't waste light.

We didn't waste water.

We didn't waste money.

If you left a room with the light on, it was like you'd committed a small crime.

"Who left the light on?"

Not a question.

A warning.

If you want to see the whole philosophy put into practice in one place, go to a grocery store.

Even the ugly vegetables get sold.

Speaking of grocery stores, you can learn a lot about people in the grocery store parking lot.

Take some time and watch what people do with their grocery carts.

Midwest etiquette is to share your cart with the next person coming in or getting out of their cars.

Wherever you shop for food, shopping carts reveal who people are.

Some people return the cart.

Some people push it onto the curb like it's a canoe.

Some people leave it in a parking space like a trap for the next innocent citizen.

And you see it and think, *so this is who you are.*

Returning a cart is one of the purest forms of doing the right thing. Nobody's watching. No reward. No trophy. You do it because it's decent.

But if you hand off a shopping cart to someone coming in the store as you are leaving, then you feel better about getting that apple pie that was not on your shopping list.

Sometimes I'll see a cart rolling toward a car in the wind and I'll catch it like I'm playing defense.

I'll park it and think, "Somebody's deductible is safe today."

It's not just to be nice, but its also practical.

But it did make you feel like a hero, even without a cape.

Hard earned money is not meant to be wasted on a $100 dent from a stray shopping cart in the grocery store parking lot.

When you grow up with a modest budget, you learn early that money has weight, not heavy and depressing, but careful. Like it should be held with two hands.

I learned it in small details: packed lunches, generic cereal, hand-me-down clothes. Not because my parents were cheap, but because they were wise.

They didn't spend money to impress people who didn't care. They spent money on what mattered: bills, food, a safe home.

Money wasn't a toy in our house. It was a tool. And tools aren't for showing off. Tools are for keeping your life from falling apart.

Nobody's impressed by a hammer.

They're impressed when the shelf stays up.

We had generic brands.

And the truth is... some generic brands are better.

But you can't say that out loud, because people get emotional about name brands. You'll start a fight in the cereal aisle.

I remember going to a friend's house and seeing the fancy cereal. The real stuff. The one with a mascot. With the shiny box. With the confidence.

I felt like I was in a museum.

I poured a bowl like I was handling a valuable resource.

I ate it slowly.

Not because it tasted better.

Because I respected the experience.

Then I went home and ate the generic cereal, and it was fine. Not tragic. Not punishment. Just cereal—doing its job.

Small things can teach you big lessons. And there were always big lessons coming from small places in the Midwest.

Most of those lessons had some part of physical labor connected to them.

Mowing lawns.

Cleaning up.

Helping a neighbor.

Odd jobs.

It's not glamorous, but it's real. It teaches you something: you can earn. You can do something useful and get paid.

There's nothing like being a kid with a lawn mower.

You feel powerful.

You feel like you own a business.

You push that mower like you're running a corporation.

Meanwhile you're sweating, the mower is half working, and you're doing math like a tiny accountant:

"If I mow three lawns a week for ten dollars each... I will have thirty dollars."

Which feels like wealth.

Thirty dollars to a kid is basically a retirement plan.

I was basically Warren Buffett, but with grass stains.

Then you realize gas costs money.

And suddenly you understand adulthood.

You understand why your dad sighed sometimes—because everything costs something.

Even the thing that earns the money.

You don't need to have a cape to benefit from a lesson like that.

And the lessons did not always involve work, sometimes they were learned by being confronted with hard decisions.

One thing I appreciate about my upbringing is this: when you mess up, you don't pretend you didn't.

You face it.

You fix it.

You learn from it.

We didn't do lying—not because we were dramatic about it, but because lying makes your life complicated.

The situation becomes a project. Complicated.

And the Midwest does not enjoy a complicated project.

I remember a moment at a store when I got too much change back.

Not a giant pile—just enough to make my stomach drop.

Because I knew it wasn't mine.

I stood there staring at the bills like they might change their mind and crawl back into the register.

And in that second, I learned something: doing the right thing isn't always hard because it's difficult.

It can be hard because it's awkward.

I didn't want to make a scene. I didn't want to embarrass the cashier. I didn't want the people behind me to sigh in that way that makes you feel like you've delayed the entire economy.

But I also didn't want to be dishonest.

So, I said, quietly, "Um... I think this is too much."

The cashier looked surprised—then relieved. They fixed it.

And that was it.

No applause.

No speech.

Just a small choice.

Everyone's life is made up of choices, some big, some small. But each with a lesson. Each choice being its own teacher.

Good teachers are part of everyday life—if you look for them. They are the quiet heroes.

Good teachers see people. They see students, hungry minds.

They notice things.

They correct you without crushing you.

In small towns, teachers sometimes know your family, which can be terrifying—because you can't reinvent yourself at school.

Your teacher might say, "How's your mom doing?" and you realize you are not invisible.

You are known and identified.

But that can be beautiful.

Because it means you're visible, seen, acknowledged.

When I was a teenager though I didn't want to be known, at least not in a large way. I would rather observe.

Speaking of school, have you ever seen a kid in class with a brand-new pencil set?

Color-coded.

Sharp.

Perfect.

I remember a new kid in our class. He was sporting a brand-new pencil set. I started struggling with pencil envy.

His pencil gang made you feel like your pencil had been living a rough life.

My pencil was short. Worn down. The eraser was tired. It looked like it had apologized too many times.

Those pencils though, they were shiny and confident—and you'd think, "Those pencils have a future."

But then the teacher said, "*Okay, quiz time.*"

I was nervous too, but that kid was stressed.

He started to panic and began twitching and then thumping one of those perfect pencils on the desk.

Those perfect pencil didn't help.

I learned another lesson: looking prepared and being prepared are not the same.

It was kind of funny to watch him squirm, but I didn't tease him about it.

The humor calmed me down for taking the test.

The Midwest doesn't do comedy like a performance.

We do comedy like a coping mechanism.

We tease with love.

I was raised with brothers and sisters and in our house, teasing was basically a second language. If we weren't picking at you a little, we were worried you might be sick.

My siblings and I always knew we were loved, and the teasing between us was part of the love—it meant you belonged and were accepted.

And that is a part of life we all share and want—acceptance.

Now—if you really want to understand Midwestern acceptance, you have to understand the wave.

Everybody knows the basic wave: one finger up off the steering wheel. Minimal movement. No drama. Efficient. Respectful. Safe.

But there's an advanced version.

It's the wave where you lift your right hand off the wheel and make a loose gesture like you're holding a baseball—fingers curled, relaxed, not trying too hard—then you do this quick angled crank motion forward and backward.

It's not big.

It's not flamboyant.

But it's friendly.

Some never use it. Too much effort. Not worth the effort.

But if you put the practice in and got the timing down, it opened to you a new level of community.

It says, "I know you, I like you, and I'm not afraid to show it."

If a farmer hits you with the advanced wave, friend... that's approval. That's like getting a gold star from a man who doesn't believe in gold stars.

As a kid, I could do the basic wave. That was fine.

But when I got my car?

That's when everything changed.

My first car was well, my first car. Not glamorous, bruised up a little but loyal.

My second car though, upgraded the driving experience. It was a '73 Chevy Impala, two-door, 454 with a 4-barrel.

I'm not going to pretend I understood every mechanical detail when I first got it. I knew enough to say the numbers with confidence and act like the numbers explained my entire personality.

"Four-fifty-four."

That's not even a sentence.

That's a declaration.

That car had weight. It had presence. It had the kind of hood that looked like it needed its own ZIP code.

And the steering wheel?

That steering wheel was basically a piece of furniture.

It wasn't one of these modern compact wheels that feel like you're controlling a video game. No, this steering wheel felt like you were captaining a ship.

And that mattered, because to do the advanced wave properly, you need leverage.

You need a wheel that stays steady when you take your hand off it.

You need a wheel that says, "Go ahead, son. Be friendly. I got us."

So, once I got the Impala, I gained the ability—not just physically, but socially—to do the advanced wave.

And when I started doing it, people started doing it back.

Not everybody.

Not strangers.

But the old-timers... the guys who looked like they'd been driving the same road since the invention of roads...

They'd hit me with that little baseball-hand crank wave.

And every time it happened, it felt like I'd been invited into something.

Not a club.

More like a quiet agreement: "We're good here. You're fine too. Keep being decent."

And if the wave is one sign of belonging, the other is the diner.

There's a diner near every small town, and it's not just a place to eat.

It's a headquarters.

It's where people go to put a soft landing under life.

They go there for breakfast and coffee and the comfort of knowing that whatever's happening in the world, the bacon is still going to show up, hot.

A real diner has an OG table.

You'll know it when you see it, because it's occupied by men who look like they've been discussing weather patterns since 1962.

When you were kids, you wanted to sit at the adult table with the rest of the grownups who were telling the stories of uncle Tom and his runaway goose.

But, when you grow up, you set your hopes on someday sitting at the OG table.

They sit in the same seats. They arrive at the same time. They speak in short sentences that carry the confidence of repetition.

The relive many of the same stories, and still have a full belly laugh at them, although the whole table and the waitress can tell the story verbatim.

You don't invite yourself to that table.

You earn your way into the orbit by being respectful and familiar and quiet enough to not disrupt the ecosystem.

It's a world of good influencers, funny stories respect and care for each other that develops groups of super friends.

Being super isn't fancy brands or generic labels—it's the small lessons that shape our choices and the people we choose to wave with.

Super doesn't require a cape.

CHAPTER 3

Static on Sundays

I was the only one in my family who really loved football.

Not "I'll watch the Super Bowl if there are good snacks" kind of love.

I mean—I loved football the way some people love a hometown—like it made sense to me. Like it was part of how I understood life.

It wasn't loud love either. I wasn't the guy painting my face and yelling at the TV like the quarterback could hear me through the screen and the laws of physics.

I was the quieter kind of fan.

The kind who watches a play and thinks, "Okay... why did that happen?"

The kind who watches a team line up and thinks, "They're about to run it, aren't they?"

The kind who learns the patterns until the game feels like a language.

It's funny, because I didn't speak many languages back then.

But football... football I could translate.

Before the snap, I'd notice down and distance, score and time, field position, personnel, formation tendencies—little cues.

And I'd think, "Alright... what would I call here?"

Sometimes I'd be right.

When I was right, it didn't make me feel like a genius.

It made me feel like a student who finally understood a lesson.

And that's the satisfaction I like.

Football became my classroom.

I watched how teams used formations to create confusion.

I watched how a good coach protected a young quarterback.

I watched how a defense disguised pressure, then revealed it at the last second.

I watched how momentum worked.

And momentum is real.

Not mystical—just human.

When a team believes, they move faster.

They tackle cleaner.

They communicate.

When a team gets discouraged, everything slows down.

Even the good players start looking ordinary.

That fascinated me.

Because it wasn't just football.

It was life.

The only problem was my body didn't match my hobby.

Our school had a great football program for football-sized people.

I was built more like a question mark.

Tall, thin, and made mostly of elbows.

If a strong wind hit me from the side, I could change zip codes.

And I don't say that for sympathy. I say it because it was true. And because it's funny now.

When you're young, you think being skinny is a temporary issue. Like someday you'll wake up and be broad-shouldered.

Then you get older and realize... no. You're just... long.

People would say, "You ever play football?"

And I'd say, "No."

And they'd look at me like, "Yeah... that checks out."

But I didn't resent it.

Because the love I had for football wasn't a love that required me to be on the field.

It was a love that made me pay attention.

And attention became my real talent.

If you've never been the only football person in your family, let me explain what that feels like.

It's like you're in a relationship with a sport.

You care deeply. You plan your day around it.

And everyone else is supportive, but they don't get it.

They'll say, "Oh, the game's on today, right?" like it's a dentist appointment.

Or they'll say, "Are they winning?"

And you'll say, "It's not that simple."

And they'll say, "Okay. Just let me know if you need anything."

That's love, honestly.

But still... it's lonely in a funny way.

It's like being the only person in your house who gets emotional about a third-and-two conversion.

So you learn early not to make people feel guilty for not caring.

You keep your passion respectful.

You celebrate quietly.

You suffer quietly.

You become the kind of fan who can carry a whole season without disturbing anybody.

Which, if you think about it, is a very Midwest way to do something.

For me, football wasn't a party. It was a ritual.

The house would be normal.

The day would be normal.

But inside me there was this calm focus like: Alright... here we go.

And then? Well, if you grew up with an old tube-style TV, you know there was only one thing certain about it.

It was certain not to consistently work.

And yes—the antenna was involved in the problem.

Because the Midwest does not always have a perfect signal.

We didn't have streaming.

We had hope.

There is a special kind of stress that comes from having a TV that requires an antenna for signal.

Our TV would sometimes act like it was doing us a favor by showing the game.

When the picture would fade out, I was the one who usually got up to "tweak" the antenna to get a better picture. Not because I understood radio waves, but because I had stock in the Sunday afternoon lesson.

My schooling was at risk.

When you are tall and lanky and start adjusting the antenna, some begin to think you are part of the antenna.

My family would spell out orders.

"Right hand up."

"Higher."

"Twist to your left."

"A little more."

So, there I'd be, doing antenna work, and the whole room would go quiet while I adjusted it.

That moment felt serious.

And then the picture would come in clear and you would hear the group in stereo to hold the antenna "right there!"

At that moment "*right there*" is not a location.

It's a lifestyle.

"*Right there*" means you have found a temporary sweet spot in a system that does not want to cooperate.

So, you freeze.

Arms up.

Back twisted.

Face serious.

And the game is playing, and you're happy, but you're also thinking, How long am I supposed to stand like this?

Because when the picture gets clear, nobody says, "Okay, you can sit down now."

They just keep watching.

And you realize your family will happily let you stand there until halftime.

They're not being cruel.

They're just being practical.

They're like, "Well... the picture's good."

And you're like, "Yes. Because I'm suffering."

That's a lesson too.

Sometimes people enjoy the result and forget the work.

That's fine.

Quiet effort doesn't always get thanked every minute.

It just keeps the picture clear.

It took a while, but we finally upgraded our TV. This one came with a remote control and cable reception.

It felt like a Neil Armstrong moment. "One small leap for the family. One giant leap for the antenna boy."

Somehow, I became the quarterback of the remote control.

Not because I wanted power.

Because nobody else wanted responsibility.

If you've ever had control of the remote in a house where nobody cares what's on, you know what kind of authority that is.

It's not celebrated.

It's tolerated.

You sit there with the remote like you're holding a steering wheel.

Everyone else is doing their own thing until they want to drive the car.

Then the rumbles begin to happen. Wrestling is inherent to teenage boys, but when you add the control of a TV remote in there, everyone gets in on that action.

I did wrestle in school for a while, which is funny because wrestling is a sport for compact people, and I was not compact.

I wasn't built like a wrestler.

I was built like a giraffe that made good choices.

Good choices are important.

When friends would come over to watch some football, I learned to test the room before I opened my mouth.

Someone would say, "Man, I love football," and I'd think, Finally. My peeps.

Then I'd say, "Nice. But do you love the game...or do you love snacks and yelling?"

Because those are two different hobbies.

Some people love football like they love a concert.

They want the crowd.

They want the noise.

That's valid.

But then there are people like me.

We love football like we love a puzzle.

We love the way it's built.

We love the moment when a team shows one thing and does another.

So, they'll say, "Who's your team?"

And I'll tell them.

And they'll say, "Oh yeah! They're great."

Then I'll say, "Yea, but—what do you think about their pass protection?"

And you can watch their eyes glaze over.

They blink like a computer restarting.

Then they say, "Ahh, Yeah... they're good."

And I say, "Nice."

And I quietly back away and go stand by the chips.

Because the chips don't judge.

That awareness helped me later in life.

Especially when my sister became a football fan.

At first, I was thrilled. I thought of the team. Our team. I thought, "finally, someone in this house speaks my language".

I started explaining things like I was a polite sports commentator who lived in the hallway.

"See how the safety is creeping down? That's a hint."

She nodded like she understood... the way people nod when you tell them about your dentist.

Then she said, "Okay, so... who is the enemy?"

That's when I realized she wasn't becoming a football fan.

She was becoming a *fan* fan. The kind with opinions, passion, and immediate rivalries—like she'd been recruited.

I said, "Well, our team doesn't really don't have any enemies—we just strongly prefer victory."

She stared at me like I'd just tried to sell her generic brand excitement.

Then she picked a team.

And of course—she picked the rival.

Not because of history.

Not because of strategy.

Not because she watched film.

She picked them because she liked their colors.

I tried to be supportive. I did. I told myself, love is bigger than the standings.

But it's hard to be emotionally mature when someone you share DNA with is cheering for your team's roughest competitor, in your own living room.

Well, technically it was my parents living room, but you get the point.

Suddenly Sunday wasn't just about getting the picture clear.

Now it was about getting the peace clear.

She'd celebrate a rival touchdown like she'd personally designed the play.

I'd sit there quietly, like a man watching someone return his shopping cart to the wrong store.

And the worst part? She was happy.

I couldn't argue with happy.

Happy is undefeated.

So, I learned to do what I'd always done: test the room before I opened my mouth.

Because nothing makes you grow up faster than realizing you can control the antenna...

but you cannot control another person's loyalty.

You can hold the remote.

You can adjust the rabbit ears.

You can even stand "right there" until your shoulder becomes a hinge.

But you can't force somebody to root the way you root.

And maybe that's the actual lesson I didn't see coming:

Sometimes "being right" isn't as important as keeping the living room livable.

So, I started doing what the Midwest does best—I served the moment.

I'd still watch closely.

Still notice patterns.

Still call plays in my head.

But now I also watched my sister—laughing, learning, getting hooked—and I thought...

Well, look at that. The signal made it through.

Super means keeping the signal clear—and even more, keeping your love clearer.

Super doesn't require a cape.

CHAPTER 4
Troubleshooting Love

In the Midwest, boyhood comes with a few standard-issue items: hand-me-down jeans that already have someone else's knees in them, a winter coat that "still fits" because nobody wants to buy another one, and the sudden realization that you now have "the right" to chop firewood—which is also an obligation, depending on whether you're the one holding the axe. You learn early that warmth is a group project, and your job is to haul the evidence.

And somewhere in the middle of all that—between stacking wood and trying to make a pair of gloves last until March—your brain locks onto mechanical machines like they're magical creatures.

Cars are the gateway, sure. But it doesn't stop there. It's tractors, mowers, chainsaws, compressors—machines with purpose. Machines with weight. Machines that look like they were designed by a man who believed work builds character and safety is mostly a suggestion.

The funny part is we didn't even have a whole lot of machinery. We weren't a "fresh toolbox, matching sockets, clean shop rag" kind of family. We were a "whatever's around that still has bolts" operation. So me and my brother turned the countryside into our personal museum of mechanical artifacts.

If a farmer had an old tractor parked behind the barn under a tarp—half covered, half forgotten—we didn't see "junk." We saw a project. If there was a car abandoned in tall grass, sun-faded and leaning like it had given up on society, we treated it like an archaeological dig. We'd climb in, grab the steering wheel, and immediately become a professional. Not trained—just confident.

It is quite amazing to see. The moment a young man starts tinkering with an engine, something happens in his head that should be studied by professionals: he becomes convinced he's an engineer. Not "learning." Not "trying." Already graduated. MIT honors. The only proof is he's holding a rusty wrench he found in the dirt and saying, "If I can just get it to breathe..." like the carburetor has feelings.

That's the Midwest version of childhood discovery: you don't need toys—you just need something heavy, something broken, and enough confidence to believe you can fix it.

And once you spend enough time crawling around dead engines and "retired" tractors, you start to notice something else: in farming communities, brands don't usually matter much. Nobody's out here ranking jeans like we're on a runway. Most of us wear whatever still fits and doesn't have a hole in a dramatic location.

But machines? Machines are different.

Because when a piece of equipment is supposed to start in cold weather, pull its weight, and not complain... you start paying attention to what it is. Not in a snobby way—more in a "this thing better work" way.

So if you grew up anywhere near farmland, there was one name you heard a lot. The green-and-yellow one. (Yes—John Deere.) Even if you weren't a farm kid, you knew what those colors meant in your area: somebody's about to do real work.

And for a lot of boys, that was the first "brand" that felt like identity—not because anyone was trying to be fancy, but because the machines were the biggest, loudest things around. When you're twelve and you've been poking around an old tractor like it's a dinosaur skeleton, the paint on the side starts to feel important—even if you don't fully understand why.

Which is why you'd see those hats pop up at school.

And here's the funny part: some of the boys wearing the green-and-yellow hat were not farm boys. They didn't know what a combine did. They didn't know the difference between hay and "just grass." But they knew the hat carried a certain vibe.

There was always that one kid who'd sit back like he'd been through some things and say, "Yeah... we been busy."

Busy doing what, bud? Your "farm" was a backyard trampoline and a grill. Your only livestock was a dog and one stubborn squirrel. But the hat made you look like you could rebuild an engine before homeroom, so... respect.

I wasn't big on tractors and balers though. The machine I really connected to was cars.

My dream was a 1967 Chevrolet Camaro RS/SS 396, 4-speed, in Cobalt Blue. Even saying it out loud feels like placing a crown on something.

I've never owned one. But even now, if I see a clean '67 Camaro, my eyes follow it like my brain is trying to remember something. And then your adult brain adds, "I would never want to insure that." That's growing up.

Besides, I was not the mechanic type. I wasn't trained how to be a mechanic.

We had working cars. Cars that took the kids to school. Cars that got you to work and home. But many of our cars were ones with a little attitude. The kind that breaks down in front of your house and turns your Saturday into a character-building event.

We had this little Mazda GLC that ran on faith and spite. That car didn't have "miles." It had "episodes."

And my dad—bless him—was one of the most loving men you could meet. The kind who would give his last shirt off his back to someone who needed it. He could troubleshoot people. He could troubleshoot situations. He could troubleshoot two boys with bad ideas before the ideas even finished forming.

But cars were not his thing.

He would "work" on a car. And that is not the same as *fixing* a car.

There is a specific type of confidence a man has when he decides he's going to fix something he doesn't understand. It's not arrogance. It's hope. It's a father looking at a problem and thinking, My family needs this solved, therefore I will attempt bravery.

One time the Mazda broke down again and my dad decided, "I'm going to fix it." He looked at the engine bay like it had personally offended him. Then he said, "Go get my tools."

When your dad says "tools," you picture a full chest. Sockets. Extensions. Stuff that clicks. Stuff that comes in a case that makes you feel official.

I came back with what my dad owned:

a hammer

a flat-head screwdriver

a pair of pliers

a flashlight

and a roll of duct tape that looked like it had survived three emergencies and a house fire

That's not a tool set. That's a starter kit for a man who is about to get humbled.

My dad took them with confidence anyway.

He tapped things.

He wiggled things.

He stared.

He made thoughtful sounds.

"Hm."

"Yeah."

"Okay."

He might've even said, "That's your problem right there," which is something men say even when they have no idea what they're looking at. It's comforting. It's also unprovable. Like a fortune cookie.

Six hours later, the tow truck pulled up.

And the tow truck didn't pull up like it was surprised to be there. It pulled up like it had been here before. Like it knew the address. Like it had family in town. It didn't even need directions—just slowed down and said, without saying it, Well... hello again.

The car was towed away and in a mechanic's garage for a few days. Repairs fixed the car, but more important, it taught me a lesson: having a hammer doesn't mean you know how to hit a nail.

My dad wasn't bitter. He wasn't embarrassed in a dramatic way. He was just... accepting. Because he wasn't trying to prove anything. He was trying to take care of us.

And that still counts.

His example motivated me to refocus on learning how to be a troubleshooter.

Troubleshooting in the Midwest often sounds like this:

The inquiry starts off, "Alright... what's it doing?"

They try to explain.

Then the troubleshooter nods slowly, like they're absorbing the facts and translating them into a prayer. Then they say, "Huh."

That "huh" can last a full minute. They look at the thing. Touch it. Listen to it. Maybe crouch for no reason, because crouching adds authority.

Then they say, "Well… it ain't supposed to do that."

And weirdly, that's comforting. Because now the problem is acknowledged. Now you're not crazy. Now you're a team.

Then they try something.

And if it works, they say, "There we go."

Not "I'm amazing." Just: "There we go." Quiet victory. Complete.

Machines taught me systems have rules.

Troubleshooting machines was not my dad's strong point, but he definitely knew when there was trouble. Honestly, if he could troubleshoot a machine the way he raised two boys, NASCAR would've called.

My dad knew where trouble was brewing with his two boys before "it" ever happened.

One day my grandfather brought a truck by that he was giving to the family.

It was an old '68 Chevy C10 longbed. My grandfather pulled in like he was delivering a gift… and a temptation. Then he and grandma took my parents out to lunch.

And while they were away, me and my brother were overcome with coolness.

Our family had not had a truck before. We were in a different league now. And conveniently, I had just gotten my driver's license—meaning I had the confidence of a professional and the experience of a potato.

So what is the natural thing two teenage boys in the country would do with a new truck?

Take it for a drive.

If you have ever lived in the country and driven on country roads, you know they become quite treacherous after newly laid gravel. Loose. Unstable. Like driving on a driveway made of marbles.

Although I know that now, back then I was still inexperienced. So in our little journey out, I was enjoying the ride, learning how to control a vehicle without power steering. Ten minutes into our venture, feeling confident, things took a turn.

Literally.

I hit a patch of newly laid loose gravel at a speed that was... let's call it "optimistic." The steering wheel decided to take over controls and whipped out of my hands, spinning to the right and then to the left. The truck followed its partner's instructions to a tee.

The truck shot up a short embankment, straddled a barbed wire fence, and came to rest on its back bumper—back wheels completely off the ground.

There we were: two boys in dirty t-shirts, staring at a truck posed like a dramatic statue called *Poor Choices*. We had just figured out our lives were shortly going to see their finality.

To face my dad was one thing.

But to face my grandfather—just a couple hours after giving my father the vehicle—well, I was in a pickle.

Unbelievably, an old farmer came driving down the road. He slowed up, looking at the scene like he'd seen it before. Slowly rolled his window down, toothpick in his mouth, and mumbled, "You boys got some trouble?"

The way he said it, I wasn't sure if he meant the truck... or our entire future.

"Yes, sir," I said. "Just a little."

"Your dad know you're out here?"

"Well... not exactly."

He paused like he was letting that truth settle into the air where it belonged.

"Well," he said, "let's see what we can do about that."

Without a few words more, he took a chain out, attached it to our axle, and had the truck out and back on the road. Then he took his chain off, put it back in his truck, shook our hands, and said, "You two be more careful now, you hear?"

I have heard those words for many years and still am learning from them.

We crawled back home with our tail between our legs. Incredibly, the truck only suffered minor scratches—mostly to the truck's dignity and our confidence.

When the time was right, we talked to dad about it.

And watching my dad and how he dealt with things like this taught me something even deeper:

He was teaching his sons while he was with them, but even while he was not.

He didn't turn it into a theater. He didn't crush us. He didn't pretend it was fine. He just handled the moment like a man who loved his boys enough to correct them and still keep them close.

His example still teaches me today.

Love shows up before it's qualified.

Love does what it can with what it has.

Super doesn't require a cape.

CHAPTER 5
Come Hug Your Father

My brother is funny in a way that doesn't always announce itself.

He's not the guy in the room telling a story with big hand motions and sound effects.

He's the guy who listens, waits, and then drops one sentence that makes you laugh so suddenly you choke a little.

But here's the thing about him: he does not like attention.

Not even good attention.

Especially not the kind that comes with affection.

If you try to compliment him, he will act like you just offered him a hot bowl of soup in a moving car.

He's going to spill it.

He's going to panic.

He's going to change the subject.

And then he's going to make fun of himself so you stop looking at him.

That's his style.

It's hilarious—and honestly, kind of admirable—because it tells you something:

He doesn't need applause.

He just wants to do the work and go home.

When we were teenagers, my brother was always the cool one.

Now, I need to clarify what I mean by "cool," because in the Midwest, "cool" can mean a few things.

Sometimes it means popular.

Sometimes it means confident.

Sometimes it means you look like you know what you're doing even when you don't.

In our family, it mostly meant this:

He didn't look like he got dressed in the dark during a power outage.

I did.

I would show up to school wearing a short-sleeve paisley button-up paired with green corduroys and tennis shoes with the sole coming off.

Not like the sole was slightly loose.

I mean it was separating from the shoe like the shoe was trying to escape my foot.

Every step sounded like a one-man broken accordion.

Flop-vroom. Flop-vroom. Flop-vroom.

It was the kind of sound that makes people turn their heads before they even see you.

Like, "Something mechanical is approaching."

Meanwhile, my brother would walk in looking like he had a sponsor.

Cool clothes.

Collar up.

Hair spiked.

The whole thing.

And I still don't know how that happened, because my mom took us to the same Goodwill store to buy our before-school clothes.

Same budget.

Same car ride.

Same aisles.

Same "try it on and see if it fits" process.

But somehow, when we walked out of there, he looked like he was headed to a magazine cover and I looked like I was headed to a lost-and-found bin.

Maybe it was confidence.

Maybe it was posture.

Maybe it was the fact that he could wear something simple and look normal, while I could wear something normal and look like a substitute teacher.

I don't know.

But the result was consistent: he looked cool and I looked... committed to comfort.

And yes, friend—I noticed.

I noticed every time my shoes made that sound.

Sometimes I would ask him straight up.

"Bro, where did you find that shirt?"

And he would shrug like he didn't know.

He'd say, "It was just there."

Just there.

That's the most annoying kind of answer, because it implies the world is full of good choices and I am simply walking past them like a blind man in a grocery store.

So then I'd replay the Goodwill trip in my mind.

I remember holding up a shirt that looked like it had survived three decades of church picnics and at least one paint project.

My mom would say, "That's fine."

And I would think, "Fine is not the same as good."

Then my brother would hold up a shirt and my mom would say, "That's nice."

Nice.

That word mattered.

"Nice" meant it looked like something a teenager would wear on purpose.

Meanwhile, I was wearing "fine," which meant my outfit was not illegal.

That's a low bar, bud.

But we cleared it.

We still talked at school.

We didn't have problems.

We were brothers.

We were close.

But our friend groups felt different.

I thought his friends were meatheads.

He thought my friends were geeks.

And, to be fair, we were both right.

But here's the funny twist:

He was a geek too.

He just looked cool while doing it.

That is a rare skill.

Some people can't be smart without showing it.

My brother could be smart and make it look casual—like he accidentally understood math.

And I did not have that skill.

If I was excited about something, you were going to know it.

I was the kind of person who could make a simple topic sound like a lecture.

He was the kind of person who could solve something complicated and then act like it was no big deal.

And as we got older, it became clear his mind was built for numbers and systems in a serious way.

Not "I got an A on a test" smart.

More like, "His brain is operating on a different program" smart.

It's not that he went on to be an accomplished mathematical scientist, but then again neither did I.

I may be a bit more comfortable with computers than him, and for me, that's my official brag for the year. But he is leaps ahead of any mechanical and engineering skills I have.

And if he heard me say that out loud, he'd immediately look down at the floor and pretend he needed to tie his shoe.

Even if he was wearing sandals.

This has stayed true about my brother from the time we were kids to now:

He does not like being the focus.

If someone gives a speech about him, he suddenly becomes interested in the ceiling tiles.

If you try to show him affection in public, he acts like you are trying to hand him a live fish.

This is not because he's cold.

He's not cold.

He's loyal.

He's thoughtful.

He's present.

He just does not want attention pointed at him like a spotlight.

He wants to stand near the light, not inside it.

And I think part of it is that he's self-deprecating.

He laughs at himself first, so nobody else can make him uncomfortable.

He'll say something like, "Oh yeah, I'm a genius," in the most sarcastic tone possible.

Then he'll immediately add, "I can't even find my keys."

It's his way of keeping everything grounded.

It's also his way of saying, "I'm not better than anyone."

Which is a healthy instinct in a world that loves to inflate itself.

Now let's talk about my dad.

My dad was affectionate.

Not in a fake way.

In a real way.

He told us he loved us.

He showed us what a loyal, loving man can look like.

He could be clumsy too—not clumsy like dropping a pencil.

Clumsy like turning around too fast and knocking over a whole display because his mind was on the conversation, not the aisle.

But he was loving.

And that love shaped us.

Here's the problem, though:

When you are a teenage boy, you do not want affection in public.

Especially not in a mall.

The mall is where teenagers go to pretend they don't care about anything.

You're trying to look calm.

You're trying to look independent.

You're trying to look like you were born knowing where the food court is.

And then your dad shows up with joy and wants to hug you.

That is not what teenage boys are emotionally prepared for.

One day we went to the mall for a family outing, and my dad was in a chipper mood.

He told us to stay near and not stray too far.

My brother gruffed at the comment—just a teenage grunt, the kind that says, "I am listening, but I would like you to know I disagree with being supervised."

My dad responded, goofy and mock-offended, "What's wrong? Don't you like being with your dad?"

Then he moved in for the hug.

And my brother reacted like a cat pouncing away from its own shadow.

He took off.

Dad gave chase.

And Dad was yelling out loud, in the middle of the mall:

"Come hug your father!"

Now, I want you to picture this.

A grown man, joyful, doing the world's least cool thing on purpose.

Teenage boy running away like he just committed a crime.

People turning their heads like, "Is this a family situation or a security situation?"

And my dad—who was not going to be defeated by teenage embarrassment—kept calling out:

"Come hug your father!"

My brother could move, too.

He was quick.

And my dad was enthusiastic, but not fast enough.

So my brother escaped.

Victory.

Or so he thought.

Because my dad returned, smiling like a man who just enjoyed a free show.

Then he looked at me.

"Give your dad a hug."

So I did.

I embraced him.

He smiled, satisfied, and said, "Well you are no fun. Not going to run away?"

I could've run.

I could've performed.

But I wasn't built like that.

I was the obedient one in that moment.

And here's the truth: I loved it.

Not because I wanted attention.

But because I felt safe with my dad.

Because his affection wasn't confusing.

It wasn't inconsistent.

It wasn't conditional.

It was steady.

It was the kind of love you don't appreciate fully until life teaches you how rare it is.

If our family had a scoreboard for that day, it would've looked like this:

Brother: 1 escape

Dad: 1 public announcement

Me: 1 full hug

Mom: 1 "y'all stop acting like that" look

And my dad would have counted it as a successful outing.

Because for him, family wasn't something you managed from a distance.

Family was something you enjoyed.

Even when it was awkward.

Especially when it was awkward.

Because awkward means real.

And real love does not wait for the perfect moment. It shows up in public. It shows up awkward. It shows up laughing—sometimes chasing you through a mall like joy has no shame.

And sometimes that love didn't chase you through a mall. Sometimes it just backed over your dreams in the driveway. Let me confess something that still visits me at two in the morning every few years.

I played trumpet in high school.

And listen—before you judge—I wanted to play drums. I wanted to be the guy in the back keeping the whole thing together, looking cool, not worrying about notes, because notes require accuracy and accuracy requires you to face the truth every time you miss one. But my mom didn't want me playing drums. She said they weren't really an instrument. I love my mom. I respect my mom. But that opinion has started debates in households with strong rhythm sections.

So I picked up the trumpet.

Learning an instrument as a young teenager is not music at first. It's noise training. It's the sound of a person discovering airflow, mouth muscles, and embarrassment all at the same time. But I stuck with it. I improved. I got to second chair out of eighteen. Second chair in a teenage mind is not just a ranking. Second chair is hope.

And then came The Day.

Morning rush. Dad taking us to school. I'm being the early-bird responsible son for once. I set my trumpet case down by the car just for a second while I run inside.

I come back out... and the car is gone.

For half a second my brain says, "They left me".

Very dramatic. Not accurate.

Then I see it.

My school-owned trumpet—crushed—on the ground.

My dad had turned around in the driveway, and that trumpet case was positioned perfectly for tragedy. He ran over it.

We got to school. The instructor looks at the trumpet the way a person looks at a totaled rental car and thinks, "So this is the energy today".

And here's the part that still makes me laugh; I had a test that day.

You might assume the test would be postponed.

No. Because the mouthpiece still fit, and technically air could still go through the trumpet.

So I performed my test on a horn that looked like it lost a fight with a tire.

The sound came out... but it was not the sound of confidence. It was the sound of consequences.

That was the day my musical dreams quietly folded up and slid into the back of my mind like an old photo. Not gone. Just archived.

And honestly, I can see now it wasn't only a loss. It was a redirect. My technical interests kept growing. I leaned into systems, devices, problem-solving—the things that fit me.

A crushed trumpet didn't ruin my life. It just humbled me in public and reminded me that sometimes the path changes in one afternoon.

And it reminded me of something else: my dad wasn't careless. He was carrying a family. He was trying to get everyone where they needed to be—and sometimes love accidentally backs over a brass instrument.

But real love is not an accident.

Real love does not wait for the perfect moment.

I want to slow down here, because humor is part of the story, but so is gratitude.

I love my dad.

Still.

The week that he fell asleep, I was able to have dinner with him and my mom.

We talked like normal.

We ate.

We were together.

And before I left, I gave him a kiss and said, "I love you."

That was the last time I saw him.

I'm not saying that to make this heavy.

I'm saying it because it is part of the reason his affection matters so much to me now.

Because when someone is gone, you don't miss their perfection.

You miss their presence.

You miss their voice in the room.

You miss the way they made the ordinary feel safe.

And you realize those embarrassing mall hugs were not embarrassing at all.

They were a gift.

They were proof you were loved without having to earn it.

So, when I think about my brother and his attention allergy, I smile.

Because I get it.

I understand the teenage instinct to run from affection.

But I also understand the adult gratitude of knowing you had a dad who cared enough to chase you down—laughing—in a mall full of strangers.

And I understand something else too:

My brother didn't want attention, but he still wanted love.

He just preferred it quiet.

He preferred it practical.

He preferred it in the form of loyalty, consistency, and being there when it counts.

That's his kind of strength.

Not loud.

Not shiny.

But solid.

And I'm grateful for him.

Super doesn't wait for a perfect moment—super hugs anyway.

Super doesn't require a cape.

CHAPTER 6

Mi Casa, My Coffee

Coffee in my family was never just a beverage. It was a language.

My dad drank coffee. My grandpa drank coffee. Not fancy. Not picky. Not doing demonstrations. They drank it the way Midwestern men do a lot of things: quietly, consistently, and without turning it into a personality.

And my mom and dad would have evenings where they played Pinochle with friends, and there would always be coffee on the table. Not as a "feature." Just as a constant—like the cards, the laughter, and that one friend who took the game a little too seriously for something you can't put on a résumé.

Coffee wasn't a treat. It was social glue. It was the warm permission slip that said, *Sit down. Stay a while. We're going to talk and laugh like we've got nowhere else to be.*

My younger sister shares my love of coffee too. And I mean shares—as in, the love is mutual, but the pot is contested territory.

One time I visited her house and she made a pot early in the morning—like she always does. Her tradition is to finish the entire pot herself, which I respect on a personal level. But now that I was visiting, it almost felt like a competition over who the coffee belonged to.

And we're a hospitality family. We grew up with that code that says, *mi casa es tu casa*. My house is your house. Come in, eat something, make yourself at home.

But sibling reality has its own version.

With coffee, my sister and I settled on: whoever gets to the pot first, wins.

Because hospitality is real... but so is caffeine.

And the truth is, we enjoy the moments coffee creates for us. Being able to get together as a family and bring each other a little gift or a homemade dish—something you made, something you thought about on the way over. But there is always coffee with it. Coffee is the part of the visit that says, *We're not just passing through each other's lives. We're here.*

Coffee out in the world is its own thing too—especially in small towns.

I love encountering coffee in restaurants and diners, the little places where you know the waitress's name and she knows yours. Or at least she knows your pattern. She sees you sit down and you can feel it in the air:

He's going to have coffee. No cream. Little sugar. Don't ask.

At these diners there aren't a lot of items to choose from. Menus are basic. There's no page devoted to "seasonal foam." You don't need a translator. You need a fork.

And the miracle of a good diner isn't the menu.

It's the refill.

The coffee isn't fancy. Nobody's swirling it and describing "notes." It's just coffee. It tastes like wake-up. You'll be mid-conversation, minding your business, and suddenly the pot appears. You look down and your cup is magically full again, and you didn't even see it happen.

Those waitresses are basically coffee ninjas. Silent. Efficient. Protective of peace.

That's customer service at its peak. And it's also a Midwest lesson hiding in plain sight: the best care is often quiet care. It doesn't interrupt your peace. It supports it.

And diners give you something else too—time. The time to sit there, sip, talk, and wait for the invite. In those places, the invite always comes. Not dramatically. Just naturally. Because coffee has a way of turning strangers into neighbors.

Now, these days coffee has... expanded.

Back then, coffee was coffee. You had regular. Maybe decaf if somebody in the family was "watching it." That was the whole menu.

Now you've got espressos, pour-overs, presses, cold brews, foams, flights, and drinks that sound like a spa treatment. I respect the craft—I really do. I'm impressed by anyone who can make a cup of coffee that tastes like chocolate and courage.

But sometimes I walk up to a counter and the choices are so specific I start to feel like I'm ordering a mortgage.

And if I need a password to order it—if I have to say something like, "Yes, I'd like the triple-whatever with the oat-something and the... uh... lavender"—then I'm not ordering coffee anymore. I'm auditioning.

Some of my friends have tried their hand at roasting coffee and selling it on the side. My buddy from Colorado decided he was going to make me his own "special roast." He brought his homemade contraption by my office and told me he'd have a roast done shortly.

I kept busy while he went to work on his recipe. I should have gotten nervous when I saw the popcorn popper come out of his box. Then I saw what looked like a device built from aluminum foil and wires and optimism.

And then the roast started.

Apparently, the process includes some smokiness—logically. But smoke in a commercial building does not mix.

The next thing you can expect is the fire alarm going off and the mandatory fire truck rolling to the scene with the captain explaining why false alarms are not good for the community—like we had personally stolen emergency services from toddlers and kittens.

From then on, my friend promised to keep his roasting outside.

That said... it was a really good cup.

Because coffee, to me, isn't a substance.

It's a moment.

Warmth in your hands when the weather is trying to prove a point. A smell that makes a kitchen feel like home. A simple pleasure that doesn't ask you to be impressive.

And then, one day, I saw coffee prepared in a way that changed my entire understanding of reality.

I was probably ten when my dad took me to visit an older couple who were longtime friends of the family. I'll call them Gladys and Jon.

Gladys ran her house with a steady rhythm. Not strict—just settled. When you walked in, you felt calm right away, like the room itself was saying, *Sit down. You're safe here.*

Gladys asked my dad if he wanted coffee.

Of course he said yes. In the Midwest, "coffee?" isn't really a question. It's hospitality. It's social glue.

Then Gladys started making it... and I watched.

She didn't use a machine.

She used a small pan.

A pan.

Like she was making soup.

She let the water heat, then poured the grounds right into the pan. A whole cup of grounds, just swimming around in there like they owned the place.

In my ten-year-old mind, coffee came from a pot. Grounds in a filter. Button. Done.

But Gladys was not concerned with my modern assumptions.

After a few minutes, she strained a cup for my dad. He accepted it happily—steaming hot and normal.

Then my dad said, "Isn't Jon going to have a cup?"

Gladys said—calm as ever—"Oh yes, but he likes his hot."

Hot?

My dad's cup was literally steaming. In my mind, steaming was the final boss of temperature. So what was "hot" if this wasn't hot?

Then Gladys did something that should be illegal.

She left the pan on the stove.

And it started boiling.

Then rolling.

Then jumping.

At this point, ten-year-old me started planning my will.

Eventually she stood up like a woman who had all the time in the world, grabbed an old glass cup—just a plain glass—and set it down in front of Jon.

And she poured that molten lava into the glass.

I'm telling you, it looked like it came out of a volcano. It was bubbling like it had emotions.

Jon picked it up like it was cold water on a summer day...

...and took a gulp.

A gulp.

Not a sip. Not a careful "test" sip. A gulp like he'd been outside mowing for three hours.

I almost fainted.

My dad didn't flinch. And that's when I realized this wasn't my first time being outclassed.

Gladys said, "Jon don't have any feeling in his throat," like she was explaining why he prefers his eggs scrambled.

Meanwhile I'm sitting there thinking:

This man is not human.

Or if he is human, he is a version of human that I am not ready for.

That might've been my first horror movie.

And somehow, it also made coffee feel... powerful.

Not just a drink.

A culture.

A preference.

A whole way of being.

Coffee at a diner is a different category. Nobody's asking what region it came from. Nobody's describing "flavor profiles." It's there to keep the conversation alive. It's hot, it's steady, and it's refilled before you ask.

It's basically a public service.

And there's comfort in that—someone quietly taking care of you without turning it into a whole production.

And maybe that's the real lesson coffee keeps teaching me, in all its forms—at my parents' Pinochle table, in my sister's kitchen, in a small-town diner, or boiling in Gladys's pan like it's trying to prove a point: coffee isn't about being impressive. It's about making room. It's about warmth, attention, and the quiet kind of care that says, I'm glad you're here, without making a speech about it.

Coffee doesn't just warm your hands—it warms the room. Super doesn't require a cape.

CHAPTER 7

You Hungry?

If you want to understand my family, don't start with the big moments. Don't start with graduations or weddings or the kind of milestones that get framed and hung up for company to admire.

Start with a kitchen.

Because in the Midwest, the kitchen isn't just a room. It's a headquarters. It's where the day begins, where the day ends, and where people who don't have the right words still find the right comfort.

This chapter is about my mom and her passion for cooking. I know that sounds like the most predictable sentence a person can write—especially if you grew up in an Italian family, where cooking is practically a love language.

But in the Midwest, it's a little different. Here it's less "romantic old-world flair" and more "a bag of potatoes and a can of flour." Same heart. Different equipment.

Mom liked garage sales, craft fairs, and painting, but more than anything I remember was her cooking.

When we were young, I swear she only had two magazines: Bon Appétit and Southern Living. And she actually cooked from them. Like a person with confidence. Like a person who believed paper could be turned into dinner.

She would take recipes from various cookbooks and—like a mad scientist—discover how to use government cheese and a chicken to become French cuisine. And I don't mean "close enough." I mean you'd take a bite and think, How did we get here from ingredients that look like they came from a budget meeting?

She watched Julia Child anytime her show came on TV, and while watching it she took copious notes like she was attending a lecture at Harvard.

The funny thing was this: Julia would be midstream explaining a process, and my mom would speak to the TV and say something like, "I wonder if she has ever tried...?" as if Julia was going to pause, look directly into the camera, and say, "Excellent point, ma'am in the Midwest—why didn't I think of that?"

Mom taught her kids to love cooking too. My two sisters and my youngest brother followed her example and are all accomplished, artisanal kitchen operators in their own rights.

I, however, was the accomplished pan and dish washer.

I never really got interested in the cooking side—though I'm extremely happy to observe, learn, and critique cooking techniques based on the taste of the palate. Give me a nice glass of Bordeaux and your best presentation of steak tartare, and I'll applaud like I paid for front-row seats and hand out compliments like tips.

Watching my mom learn from Julia Child and then teach her children the love of cooking was genuinely enjoyable. Her daughters were her sous chefs, and she was the executive chef of the household.

And the output of that kitchen wasn't just food.

It was atmosphere.

You can learn a lot about a family by watching what happens when someone walks through the door at an unexpected time.

Some homes say, "What do you need?"

My mom's home says, "Sit down. You look hungry."

My mom can cook. And when I say she can cook, I don't mean she follows a recipe and hopes for the best. I mean she can make food that feels like a memory, even if you've never tasted it before.

She can take ordinary ingredients and turn them into something that makes you pause mid-bite and realize you're calmer than you were five minutes ago.

If you come over to her house, you are going to eat. It's not a question. It's not a suggestion. It's a fact.

In my family, you don't get to say, "No thanks, I'm fine," and think the conversation is over. Because "I'm fine" is not a real sentence to a Midwestern mom.

"I'm fine" just means, "I have not yet been properly fed."

So she'll look at you, nod slowly, and keep cooking anyway.

Then she'll serve you "just a little," which will be a plate that could sustain a small construction crew. And she'll do it with the calm confidence of a person who has been doing this since before you knew what hunger was.

I grew up thinking this was normal. I thought every household ran on a steady cycle of coffee, meals, and leftovers that mysteriously multiplied overnight.

Then you get older, you travel, you meet other families, and you realize: not everyone's mom feeds the entire county.

Some people have a "food plan."

My mom has a food reflex.

Let me explain something about my mom's refrigerator.

It is not a refrigerator.

It is a time capsule. It is a museum of containers. It is a miracle of Midwestern management.

If you open the fridge at my mom's house, you might think she's preparing for a small winter storm, even if it's July.

There will be leftovers.

There will be a bowl covered in foil that nobody is allowed to throw away because, "That's still good."

There will be a container with a lid that does not match, but it works anyway because my mom is not picky about plastic.

And there will always be something that makes you say, "What is that?"

And my mom will answer without looking, "Oh, that's for tomorrow."

Tomorrow.

My mom plans meals the way farmers plan fields. She thinks ahead. She knows people will show up. She doesn't cook just for the people currently sitting in the room. She cooks for the people who might appear later.

That is love with a budget and a brain.

And if you've ever been to a house where nobody seems prepared for anything, you understand how comforting that is. It's like walking into a place where someone already thought about you before you arrived.

Here's something else about my mom.

She has health problems.

I don't say that for sympathy. I say it because it makes her steady care even more meaningful.

Pain has a way of shrinking life. It makes people withdraw. It makes them conserve energy. It makes them start saying, "I can't," even when they don't want to.

My mom has learned to be wise about her limits.

But she also has a quiet stubbornness that keeps showing up.

She still makes time. She still cooks. She still cares.

Not like she's trying to prove something—like she's refusing to let difficulty steal her humanity.

That kind of bravery doesn't get celebrated enough because it doesn't look dramatic.

It looks like a woman getting up, moving a little slower, and doing the next right thing anyway.

Sometimes strength looks like an apron and a steady hand.

After my father died, our family changed. Loss changes a home. It changes the calendar. It changes the sound of the day. It creates a silence in places that used to be filled with familiar routines.

But one thing I admire about my mom is that she did not choose to isolate.

She has "her girls." That is what she calls them.

A group of women she spends time with—friends who check in, laugh, drink coffee, and talk about life like normal people who have carried real things and still want to be joyful.

If you have never watched older women laugh together after they've been through hard seasons, you are missing one of the healthiest sights on earth.

They don't laugh because life is easy.

They laugh because they're alive.

They laugh because they know what matters now.

They laugh because, at some point, you realize you are not supposed to carry grief alone.

You carry it with people.

That's what friends are for.

And that's what my mom's "girls" are. Not a replacement for family—a support system that keeps a person upright.

I respect that, because there is a temptation—especially in the Midwest—to act like you're fine even when you're not.

My mom has the courage to stay connected.

She also has a habit of texting one simple question:

"You hungry?"

Now, that is not a normal question. Because the answer is always yes. Even if you are full, a Midwestern mom can make you hungry with the suggestion of food.

So when she texts, "You hungry?" what she is really saying is:

"I thought about you."

"I have something ready."

"You can come here and feel okay."

That is love in two words.

Not fancy.

But powerful.

And when you have that kind of steady love in your life, it shapes the way you treat other people. You stop seeing hospitality as a performance and start seeing it as a responsibility. A quiet responsibility. The kind you do because it's right. The kind you do without needing credit.

If you want to see therapy the Midwestern way, watch a group of women with coffee.

They are not sitting down to solve global problems. They are not writing policy. They are not announcing life lessons.

They are just talking.

And somehow, by the end of it, people are lighter.

There will be a cup of coffee. There will be a dessert someone brought "just because." There will be a story about somebody's grandkids. There will be at least one comment like, "I don't know what's wrong with people these days," followed by a laugh that says, "But we are still here."

And there will be a moment where you can feel the room breathe.

That is community.

Not flashy.

Not online.

Just real.

And real is what keeps people going.

When people write about their childhood, they often focus on events. I think the setting matters just as much.

My mom's kitchen shaped my understanding of care. It taught me love can be practical and still be deep. It taught me feeding people is not just about food. It's about attention. It's about welcome. It's about saying—without big speeches—"You belong here."

And that message becomes part of you.

Later in life, when you have your own home, you realize you want the same atmosphere. You want people to relax. You want hospitality to be normal, not performative.

That's one of the reasons my wife's home means so much to me. Different style. Same value.

I can see the thread. It starts with my mom's kitchen and continues into my marriage. That's how family works. It passes down a certain tone. A certain warmth. A certain steadiness.

And if you didn't grow up with it, you can still build it.

You learn it. You choose it. You practice it until it becomes the way you live.

Super is a kitchen that says, "You belong here."

Super doesn't require a cape.

CHAPTER 8

She Doesn't Wear a Cape

Some people decorate a house. My wife builds a home. That sounds like a greeting-card sentence, but I mean it like a measurement. If you live with her long enough, you start noticing the difference between "nice" and "nourishing." Nice is what you can point to. Nourishing is what you feel in your body when you walk in the door. A home can look perfect and still feel tense. Another home can look simple and still feel like your body finally got permission to unclench. My wife has that gift. Not because everything is expensive. Because everything is cared for. Her order is quiet. It doesn't announce itself. It doesn't beg for attention. It just says, without words, you're safe here.

Every guest has the same moment in the doorway. They pause. They look at their shoes. They look at our floor. Then they look back at my wife like she's holding the answer in plain sight. "Do you want me to take my shoes off?" My wife answers the same way every time, calm and warm: "Whatever you're comfortable with." Which sounds easy... until you realize the guest didn't come to be comfortable. The guest came to be correct. So they stand there doing moral math with footwear. And I get it. I'm from the Midwest. In the Midwest, taking off your shoes isn't just hygiene—it's a statement. It says, "I respect your carpet." It says, "I'm not dragging my whole day into your peace." If you grew up around farms, it also says, "Let's not talk about where I've been." Most people take them off. My wife gives them the same warm smile either way. No extra approval. No punishment. Just steady welcome. That steadiness is part of why she feels like home to me.

My wife has a look she gives me that can lower the volume of the whole world. She'll look up, there's that little twinkle in her eye, she tilts her head ever so slightly, and she squeezes a cute smile that makes her cheeks puff pink. It's the kind of smile that doesn't demand anything from you. It just offers you something. Like, "Hey. Come back to the room. I'm here."

And she's creative in a way that feels like a quiet superpower—because it's not just talent, it's patience. One time she made a stop-motion video called Coffee Time for a talent show with friends. And she does not like performing in front of people if she doesn't have to, so she performed the only way that felt comfortable: by making something so good it did the talking for her. She took hundreds of pictures—hundreds—of coffee beans crawling out of their bag, running around a cup, and jumping in like a troupe of circus ants. Then the spoon, milk, and sugar all came alive, and the whole thing played against Natalie Cole in the background like we were suddenly watching a tiny coffee musical. It was hilarious and impressive and so detailed that I realized something: she doesn't just "make things." She makes things right.

That's been in her since she was a kid. She loved to draw—but only if she didn't go out of the lines. Which tells you everything you need to know about her: she has an insatiable drive to make things look amazing and perfect for other people. From decorating for gatherings to making our guest room feel like a Four Seasons retreat, she puts care into the small things that people think "just happen."

My wife's house is clean, yes—but it isn't nervous-clean. It's not a performance. It's not stress in a nicer outfit. It's care. When she folds a blanket, she's making a landing place. When she wipes a counter, she's handing the next person a calmer tomorrow. I didn't grow up with that kind of quiet consistency. We weren't slobs. We were Midwestern functional. If the sink was full, you did dishes. If company was coming, you cleaned like your aunt had already turned onto your street. My wife's rhythm is different. It doesn't spike. It doesn't crash. It just continues. And living inside that rhythm changes you.

Especially if you marry a tech guy. Because tech guys don't see clutter the same way. We see tools. We see "future solutions." We see twelve cords and think, "That's preparedness". My wife sees twelve cords and thinks, "We are being invaded by plastic spaghetti".

Early in our marriage, I stored tech supplies the way my brain stores ideas: everywhere, on purpose, for no reason. A charger on the couch. A charger in the car. A charger in the kitchen drawer. A charger in a bag that also contains three other bags. A charger in a pocket I forgot existed. To me, this was a network of readiness. To my wife, it looked like our house was slowly being annexed by white cords.

One day she held up a charger and asked, sweetly, "Is this yours?" If you've been married longer than six minutes, you know that question isn't really about the charger. It's about the future. So I said, "Yes." She smiled. "Where does it go?" And my mind went blank. Because in my world, chargers don't go anywhere. Chargers simply appear when needed, like raccoons. So I told the truth. "I don't know." She nodded like a person who has found the root issue without raising her voice. Then she solved it the way she solves most things: calmly, kindly, permanently. She bought a basket. She set it down and said, "Tech goes here."

And at first, it felt restrictive. Tech guys don't love boundaries. We like options. But then I realized the basket wasn't a punishment. It was mercy. Because now I wasn't searching for my own stuff like I was playing hide-and-seek with myself. And our home stayed peaceful. We both won.

My wife has a quiet radar for people. If she knows you like coffee, she offers it. If she knows you run cold, a blanket appears. If you look tired, the house gets softer—less noise, less pressure, more room to breathe. She doesn't announce it. She doesn't make you thank her with a speech. She just does it.

I used to think hospitality was "having people over." Now I think hospitality is making someone feel like they're not in the way. We've had guests say, "Oh don't worry about me, I don't want to be a burden." My wife always answers the same way: "You're not a burden." Then she proves it. Not with fuss. With attention. She serves without needing credit, which is rare in a world where people want points for kindness.

Being married to someone like that is like living next to a lighthouse. You don't get yelled at to change. You just keep steering toward the light. There is a kind of love that tries to change you by pressure. This is not that. My wife's love says, "You're safe. Now grow." And that changes everything.

And when I'm deep in thought—when I'm lost in a problem, over-occupied, mentally three rooms away—she doesn't scold me back into reality. She supports me. A little treat appears like it was dropped into the scene from nowhere. Or a breakfast sandwich gets packed for us when we're running too early, too fast, too late to stop and sit down like normal adults. That's her loyalty. It's not flashy. It's not loud. It's love that shows up quietly and keeps the day from falling apart.

Because I have flaws. I'm lanky. I overthink. I can turn a simple plan into a spreadsheet. I can pack three chargers and forget socks. She doesn't mock me. She laughs with me. She helps me. And she expects me to be a man—not perfect, but faithful. The kind of man who protects peace at home in small ways: listening, apologizing, doing the next right thing when nobody's clapping.

Super is the quiet look that says, "I'm with you."

Super doesn't require a cape.

CHAPTER 9

The Printer is Not the Problem

My path into tech wasn't flashy. It was practical. It was the kind of practical that shows up with a calm face and stays until the problem stops misbehaving.

I grew up around enough "barely working" to appreciate "works cleanly." Technology wasn't a toy in my world. It was more like a fancy spoon—shiny, helpful, and technically optional. We were raised on forks. A computer felt... extra.

Still, whenever I got a chance to sit down at one, I took it. Lunch breaks. After school. Borrowed time. Stolen minutes between life and responsibility. Any moment I could trade comfort for learning, I did.

And if you learned tech the way I did, you know the main curriculum is this sentence:

"Well... that wasn't the plan."

You click one thing and three other things happen. You type a password you know is right, and the computer politely calls you a liar. You stare at the screen like it just insulted your whole family.

Then you learn something humbling: a lot of tech problems aren't about "broken." They're about "assumed." And assumptions... that's where tech gets everybody.

Somewhere along the way, life handed me an unexpected door. I met a man from Ghana—sharp, disciplined, calm. The kind of person who doesn't panic when things go sideways. He was helping build a training program for inner-city high school graduates—teaching telecom basics, central-office work, and the kind of skills that turn a job into a future.

I wasn't from that background, and I wasn't aiming for telecom, but his vision hooked me. Not because of the tech—because of the teaching. He had this steady way of equipping people without making them feel small. And my mind embraced it like a warm fleece blanket at a December game in Buffalo. It fit. Everything clicked.

Watching him taught me something more important than cabling colors: technology is not magic. It's patterns. It's cause and effect. It's logic... with wires.

If something isn't working, it's usually not because the device woke up and chose violence. It's because something is missing, misconfigured, misunderstood, unplugged, or—this one is the most common—the power strip is turned off.

That last one is basically the Midwest tech support anthem.

From there I started learning networking, routers, fiber, systems—how invisible things connect visible things. And slowly, without announcing it, I became the guy people called.

Not because I wanted attention.

Because somebody had to.

And that's when I learned the truth about tech support: you don't choose the work. The work chooses you.

One of the first times I helped a good friend with a printer, I didn't realize I wasn't fixing a device—I was enlisting in a war. Because it's never just one printer. It's an entire extended family of printers. Different sizes, different personalities, different ways of failing, all showing up at the worst possible times—right when you're finishing a project, heading out the door, or finally trying to go to sleep.

This first episode seemed innocent. My friend had a lecture ready and needed it printed. Simple. And this was before Wi-Fi entered the world and brought a whole new branch of chaos with it. This printer was old-school: cable to computer, handshake of partnership, nothing romantic—just business.

Except the printer didn't want business.

First it was the drivers. Then the operating system decided it had opinions. Then came the paper jam that wasn't there—like the printer was accusing us on principle. Then, just as we started making progress, it ran out of ink. All of this happened before we could get three little pieces of paper to print.

My friend—an older man with limited remaining hair—looked like he was about to donate the rest of it to the floor.

In the end, I took the file on a jump drive to a local print shop and paid actual professionals to do what our home equipment refused to do: quietly behave.

But that day lit something in me. Not anger—purpose. Because what people need in that moment isn't a tech wizard. They need someone calm in the room who can say, "You're not crazy. This is just what printers do sometimes."

That's when I started noticing something: people don't call you because they love technology. They call you because they love peace.

Most people aren't afraid of devices. They're afraid of feeling small. A printer doesn't just "not print." A printer makes a capable adult feel powerless. Now they're one paper jam away from moving to a cabin where nothing beeps.

That's the real issue.

Not the device.

The shame.

Here's what I learned early, and it changed everything: calm first. Skill second. Because fear wipes the memory clean. People forget what they clicked. They stop listening. They start guessing. And when grown adults guess under pressure, they don't guess small. They guess like a person trying to defuse a bomb with a spoon.

That's why tech support starts with safety—not therapy safety. Practical safety. The kind where someone can breathe and say, "I don't understand this," without feeling judged.

There's a specific tone people use when they're about to admit they clicked something. They lean in. They lower their voice. They look around like the laptop might be listening.

"Okay... so... I clicked something."

Then they add, like it's a confession:

"And I don't know what it did."

And then the final line, whispered like a courtroom verdict:

"And I think I ruined it."

I learned to answer the same way every time.

"Okay. Good news. You probably didn't ruin anything."

You can watch the panic come down. Their shoulders drop like you just turned off an alarm.

Then I add:

"And even if you did... we can fix it."

Now they're ready to learn.

Tech knowledge can inflate your ego if you let it. People react to simple fixes like they're wizardry. You turn something off and back on, and they stare at you like you just cured a disease.

And if you're not careful, you start liking that look. You start liking being needed.

That's how you become "that guy."

"That guy" makes people feel dumb so he can feel smart. "That guy" uses big words when small words would work. "That guy" turns every question into a performance.

I didn't want to be that guy.

So I tried to build a different kind of confidence. Not microphone confidence—service confidence. The kind where you don't need to prove you're smart, because the goal isn't to look smart. The goal is to make the room feel capable again.

And here's the part that surprised me: football was training me for troubleshooting.

Because football taught me to stay calm under pressure, read what's happening, adjust, and do the next right thing—without blaming everyone on the team.

Tech is the same.

One huge mistake new teachers make is teaching features instead of outcomes. They'll say, "Here's the app, here's the menu, here's the settings..." Meanwhile the person is thinking:

"I just want to see pictures of my granddaughter without accidentally sending them to the entire planet."

So I learned to ask one question that saves everything:

"What are you trying to do?"

Not "What's wrong?"

What are you trying to do.

Because outcomes are human. I want to communicate. I want to remember. I want to stay connected. I want to feel safe. I want to not mess this up.

That's everyone.

And when you teach from the outcome, people don't just learn faster—they feel dignity come back online.

The longer I worked in tech, the more I realized the real work wasn't devices.

It was dignity.

Helping someone learn technology is helping them keep up with life. Helping them stay independent. Helping them not feel left behind. And you can crush that with one impatient sentence.

So I tried to keep my teaching simple:

Calm

Kind

Clear

Respectful

And a little funny

Because humor relaxes people.

And once they relax, they learn.

Super is restoring calm before fixing the problem.

Super doesn't require a cape.

CHAPTER 10
The Sync People

I grew up loving Apple computers the way some kids loved sports cars.

Not to show off—just because I could tell it was made with care.

Even as a kid, I noticed when something was designed on purpose—simple, clean, and strangely polite.

It looked like that from a distance.

The problem was: I couldn't afford it.

So for a long time, it was a window-love. The kind where you stand outside a bakery with gum money, respectful admiration in your heart, studying the frosting like it's art and thinking; "Someday..."

And that "someday" sat in me for years—not as bitterness. More like a quiet goal that behaved itself. Because in the Midwest, even your dreams are supposed to act polite in public.

Some people love that brand because it's trendy. Some people love it because it's expensive. Some people love it because it's what they've always used.

For me, it was simpler: it felt like the opposite of chaos.

I grew up around enough "barely working" to develop a deep respect for "works cleanly." Cars that needed a prayer. TVs that needed antenna miracles. Little systems that required patience and a calm tone. So the idea of something that just worked—and didn't look angry while doing it—felt comforting. It felt like peace you could plug in.

The first time I saw a Mac up close, I didn't react like a normal person.

Normal people see a computer and think, Okay, computer.

I saw a Mac and thought, This is furniture.

It looked like it belonged in a clean home. It looked like it wouldn't argue with you. Like the kind of device that says, "We're going to do this the right way, and we're not going to panic." Meanwhile, the computers I was used to were more like: "Aw, bless your little heart."

Here's the funny part. I couldn't afford them but somehow... I always ended up with an iPhone.

Not in a flashy way. More in a "how did this happen again?" way—like life kept shuffling the deck and sliding one into my hand. Sometimes it was used. Sometimes it was old. Sometimes the battery had more of a personality than a lifespan. But it was an iPhone.

Buying a used iPhone gives you a very adult kind of confidence—until lunchtime, when the battery starts negotiating.

By lunch it's acting tired, like it put in a full shift and would like to go home.

And you don't even complain much—because you chose this. That's adulthood: gratitude and chargers.

But the device gave me the opportunity to feed my tech.

You see, you don't wake up one day and decide, I am a tech person.

You work into it with a hunger to learn and an insatiable desire to push buttons, pull levers, and make things click.

In reality, most young boys have that desire. It only needs to be honed and directed.

When I was able to get an iPhone, I fed that desire. I pushed, poked, and yanked on every button available. And through the experience, knowledge developed.

A person told me once that a consultant is nothing more than a person with one step on your knowledge—and the smarts enough not to show his cards.

So opportunities happened that allowed me to use what I was taught to teach others.

I just kept becoming the guy people called when something didn't work.

It started small—family members saying, "Hey, can you look at this?" And I'd look at it and start asking questions. Not accusatory questions. Troubleshooting questions.

"What changed?"

"What happened right before it stopped?"

"Is it plugged in?"

That last one is important. A shocking percentage of modern suffering is power-related.

Low-battery. Dead battery. Battery not charging.

Words that start your heart racing the same way as driving a car and getting a flat at 55.

And as I fixed a few things, a pattern formed. People noticed I didn't panic. I didn't make them feel dumb. I didn't act superior. I just worked the problem.

That calm had to come from somewhere. Turns out, it already had a training program—years of little drills in everyday life. Football helped, sure. But so did growing up around things that needed figuring out, working with your hands, and learning to stay steady when something wasn't going right.

Because troubleshooting is basically calm observation while everyone else is emotionally sweating. You don't guess loudly. You don't make it about you. You ask what changed. You check the basics. You keep your tone steady so the person in front of you stays steady too.

And the Midwest had been training me for that long before I knew what to call it. Stay calm. Don't exaggerate. Do the next right thing. Fix what you can. Ask for help when you need it. Don't lie to cover a mistake. Those values translate perfectly into tech.

And yes—printers still lie with the confidence of a man who has never been audited. But that's a different chapter. That's a whole different emotional budget.

Somewhere between helping family and rescuing friends, I crossed into a new category: strangers who believed I was "a tech person" on purpose.

Years after being the kid who admired that clean design from a distance, I ended up doing tech work for a man in Palm Beach—an older gentleman with more money than most towns and a personality that was eccentric in the harmless way.

In Palm Beach, people are friendly but careful. They'll smile and invite you in, but they also want to know who you are before they hand you anything important.

And in Palm Beach, your phone is important. Not because it's expensive—because it's personal. It's your calendar, your pictures, your finances, your travel plans, your family group chats, your memories... and the one number you can't lose: the plumber you trust.

My phone rang one afternoon and a polite voice asked, "Are you the Apple person?"—like that was a licensed profession.

I said, "Yes sir. How can I help you?"

There was a pause that felt like a door lock clicking into place.

Then he said, "Before we schedule anything, my office will run a background check on you."

I wasn't offended. I was impressed.

He continued, "It is a ninety-point check."

Ninety points. I didn't even know a background check could have that many points. I thought a background check was basically: *Is he dangerous? No? Okay.*

So I asked, because curiosity is part of my condition: "What are the points?"

He replied, dead serious, "We check everything."

He said it like a judge. Then he just sat there—like I was supposed to feel guilty about something I hadn't done yet.

That was the whole answer: everything.

A day later I received an email with forms. Lots of forms. The questions started normal—name, address, past addresses, references—and then got personal in a way that makes you sit up straighter.

Have you ever used another name?

Have you ever lived outside the country?

Have you ever been terminated for cause?

That one made me smile. I wanted to write, "No, but my high school basketball coach did not love me." That's not termination. That's just life.

I filled it out honestly, because I don't want a life where I have to keep track of my stories. Truth is simple. Truth is portable. Truth lets you sleep well.

A week later his assistant called and said, "You are cleared."

Cleared. Like I was about to work on a space shuttle.

And in a way, I was—because for him, his devices were how his life moved. If they didn't sync, his world didn't flow.

When I arrived at his home, I expected something flashy. Instead it felt quiet. Tasteful. Like the house wasn't trying to show off, but it also wasn't trying to pretend.

His assistant said, "He likes things done a certain way."

I smiled and said, "No worries. I like things done a certain way too."

That was true. Mine is just cheaper.

I walked into his office and he stood up, looked at me, and said, "You are tall."

That was his first observation.

I said, "Yes sir. The Lord did that one."

He studied me for another second, like height might affect syncing.

He nodded like he was considering the design.

Then he slid an iPhone across the desk like we were about to play cards and said, "It is not syncing."

So I went into my calm routine. I handled his phone respectfully. I didn't tap around randomly. I narrated in plain language—because competence is comforting, but clarity is calming.

"This is your Apple ID."

"This is your iCloud setting."

"This is your storage."

"This is why it's not syncing."

"This is how we fix it."

He nodded slowly the whole time.

Then he asked a question that was so simple it was brilliant: "How do I keep this from happening again?"

That's a wise question. A lot of people want a quick fix. Wise people want a system.

So I gave him a system—just a few habits that keep life steady. Update at calm times. Back up regularly. Keep passwords organized. Don't ignore storage warnings like they're polite suggestions.

He sat back and said, "Good."

Then he looked at me and said, "You are honest."

Not "you are smart." Not "you are talented." Honest.

And in that office, I learned something that stuck with me: trust is the real luxury.

Before I left, he walked me to the door himself. At the threshold he paused and said, "One more thing."

He led me back to his office and opened a drawer full of chargers. All identical. All lined up.

"I keep extras," he said.

Then he opened another drawer. More chargers.

Then another. More chargers.

He looked at me and said, "I do not like surprises."

Then, with total seriousness: "If Apple stops making these, I will need to buy whatever is still on the market."

I didn't know what to say to that, so I said the only honest thing.

I responded, "Then you will need a warehouse."

Then I added, "But then... I don't think you'll have trouble buying a warehouse."

He laughed. A real laugh.

And that was the moment I remembered: wealth doesn't remove humanity. It just changes the price tag on what you worry about. Same nervous system. Different furniture.

And once you help one wealthy man sync his life, the universe decides you're qualified to fix everyone else's phone at a cookout.

If you want to know when you have officially become "the tech guy," it's not when you fix your first computer.

It's when you're at a perfectly normal social gathering—food, laughter, someone telling a story too long—and a person approaches you with the expression of someone who has been carrying a secret.

They smile, but it's tight.

They lean in like they're sharing classified information.

"Hey bud... can I ask you something real quick?"

That sentence is never quick. It's a soft opening to a full appointment disguised as casual conversation.

And I don't blame them. Tech problems feel small until they get personal. It's not the phone. It's what the phone holds: family messages, calendars, photos, passwords, reminders, the ability to feel included.

So when the phone misbehaves, people feel like they misbehaved.

My job wasn't to fix a device.

My job was to keep it light and keep it kind.

If they could relax, they could remember what they did.

If they could remember what they did, we could fix it.

And there's always a moment at gatherings when you realize you helped one person... and now there are two or three others nearby pretending they are not waiting. They drift closer every time you say, "There we go."

At first, you think, "Wow. I'm useful."

Then you realize this is how plumbers feel.

Because as soon as the room discovers you can fix something, you become a public utility.

The way people hand you a phone tells you everything.

Some people hand it to you carefully, like it contains their entire life.

Some people hand it to you fast, confident, like a toddler handing you a sticky toy.

And some people don't hand it to you at all. They hover.

Those are the ones I always feel for, because they aren't guarding the device from you. They're guarding their dignity from the situation.

So I talk them through it gently.

"Okay ma'am, tap right there."

"Alright bud, swipe up."

"Perfect. You're doing it."

And you can watch bravery come back in real time.

That's the part I love.

Not the fix. The courage.

The Settings app on an iPhone is one of the strangest places a human can visit. The word "settings" sounds friendly, like you're adjusting comfort. But inside, Settings feels like a storehouse where everything is labeled by someone who already knows where it is.

There's a section called General.

General isn't a setting. It's the system saying, "We ran out of categories."

Inside General there's something called About.

About what?

About your phone.

Then you discover the search bar inside Settings—and it's the most honest feature ever put in a modern device. Because that search bar is the phone admitting, "Nobody knows where anything is. We're done pretending."

And just when you think you've found what you need, your phone hits you with the next level: security.

Two-factor authentication is a good idea. It protects people. It keeps information safe. But emotionally it can feel like this:

You can't sign in because you need a code.

The code is sent to the device you can't access.

That's like locking your keys in your car and the car saying, "Show me your keys."

So people start talking to the phone like it's a stubborn relative.

"Why would you do this to me?"

"I'm the owner."

"We have been through so much together."

And I don't laugh at them. Because we are all one forgotten password away from humility.

Two-factor is the lock. Apple ID is the part where the lock asks for your birth certificate.

Then there's the Apple ID identity crisis.

Nothing makes a person feel more unsure than an Apple ID prompt. It's not asking, "What's your password?" It's asking, "Who are you, really?"

People will say, "I never made an Apple ID."

Yes you did.

You made it years ago with the TV on and someone talking to you and you just wanted to get to the home screen. You created it with hope and confusion—like most modern agreements.

So we reset it. We write it down in a way that makes sense. Not on a sticky note that disappears into a drawer of coupons. Somewhere safe. Somewhere you'll actually look.

Because organization is kindness aimed at your future self.

The simplest fixes often get the biggest gratitude. You tap one setting. You turn off one mode. Suddenly the whole world is back. And the person looks at you like you performed a rescue mission.

At first, that feels awkward—because you know it wasn't dramatic.

But then you realize what they're grateful for isn't the button. It's the calm. It's the way you didn't make them feel small. It's the way you made the problem feel solvable.

And somewhere in all of that—phones, settings, background checks, and drawers full of chargers—I started noticing a shift in myself.

At first, I was just the guy who could help.

Then I became the guy who could explain.

And after that, I started learning how to build habits and systems that kept people from needing a rescue in the first place.

I used to think being helpful meant swooping in with a quick fix. But the real upgrade was learning to give people a system—simple habits that keep life steady: backups, updates at calm times, passwords written down like you respect your future self.

Anyone can do a rescue. A steady person teaches prevention. That's the difference between being "handy"... and becoming trustworthy.

Super doesn't require a cape.

CHAPTER 11

My Emotional Support Tech

Moving to Palm Beach didn't magically turn me into a business owner.

There was no welcome packet that said, "Congrats, friend—here's your client list and a free office."

I didn't have the money to start a business the way people picture starting a business. No fancy logo package. No cash cushion. No "brand strategy meeting" where everybody drinks sparkling water and says words like synergy.

What I had was a conscience.

And sometimes a conscience will interrupt your whole plan.

My tech brain was in gear and doing well. But something was missing.

Working every day, fixing problems directly with computers, switches, and devices was not giving me the satisfaction I thought it alone would. I began noticing when I was really enjoying my work. People.

When I was doing my thing and fixing problems, bad Wi-Fi signal, firmware updates, command line additions, everything was clicking. But it wasn't feeling. The human need gave me the spark to make a move. I needed to use my tech to teach.

One day I came home, stood in the kitchen, and told my wife, "I quit my job."

That sentence sounds bold when you tell it later. In the moment, it felt less like boldness and more like obedience—like stepping over a line you'd been staring at for weeks and finally admitting, *I can't do that and still sleep well.*

Principles aren't decorations. They're load-bearing beams. You pull them out and the house might look fine for a little while... but eventually something sags.

My wife didn't yell. She didn't insult me. She didn't shame me.

She froze for half a second—and I could see the math start happening behind her eyes.

Not angry math. Responsible math. The kind a steady person does when she loves you and also enjoys having electricity.

Then she said, very softly, "Okay... why?"

That question is what a strong marriage sounds like. Not, "What is *wrong* with you?"

Rather, "Help me understand."

So I told her the truth, plain and simple: "I can't compromise my principles."

That sentence can sound proud if you say it like a trophy. I didn't mean it like that. I meant it like a warning label—because I know myself. If I betray my conscience, I lose my peace. And if you lose your peace, you start becoming a different person.

I didn't want to become a different person. I wanted to become a better one.

My wife listened—and then she did something that still makes me love her more every time I remember it.

She supported me.

Not because it was comfortable. Because it was right.

To be clear, she did have what I would call a mild panic moment. Not dramatic. More like a silent storm. She got very still and started asking practical questions like a person holding a rope in a windy place.

"Okay. What's the plan?"

Now, I had a plan in the way young men have plans—meaning: I had confidence and three ideas. Confidence is not a plan. Confidence is a mood.

So I said, "I'm going to start my own business."

She nodded slowly, like she had just accepted news that would require prayer and maybe a budget spreadsheet.

Then she asked, "With what?"

And this is where my entrepreneurial story becomes very Palm Beach and very humble at the same time.

"With my phone."

Because that's what I had. No office. No staff. No fancy equipment. Just a device, a brain that likes solving problems, and the belief that if I serve people well, the work will grow.

That belief isn't magic. It's just the old Midwest idea of doing honest work and letting it speak for itself.

So I started with something that felt natural to me: I taught.

I built a simple tutorial—step-by-step, plain language, the kind of language that wouldn't shame a person for not knowing something. I didn't want to sound like a manual. I wanted to sound like a friend who knows where the buttons are.

What is Wi-Fi?

How do you close an app?

How do you find photos?

How do you video call without fear?

What do you do when something feels "stuck"?

Then I went to the local library and asked if I could use a room.

They said yes.

Then they said, "We can put it in the monthly newsletter."

I did not understand the power of a library newsletter in a beach town. I thought it was a cute little paper people glanced at.

Wow, was I wrong.

A library newsletter in Palm Beach is basically a broadcast network. It is trusted. It is official. It is the paper retirees read with coffee and a pen, circling activities like they're planning a cruise.

So they listed my class: Free Tablet Basics.

Here's the funny part: I didn't even own the exact tablet I was teaching. I taught the class using my phone and the library projector. The layout was close enough to teach the logic—and logic is what people actually need.

When the room filled up, I saw the same expression on a lot of faces: hope mixed with fear. They were holding their devices the way you hold a valuable dish you don't want to drop.

So I started with permission.

"Okay sis, okay bud—today we're going to learn the basics. And I want you to know something: you can't break it by touching it."

That line always gets a laugh because it sounds brave.

But it's also true. Most of the fear is unnecessary—and fear is what keeps people from learning.

Then the questions started.

And the funny thing is, the questions were never only about technology.

They were confessions.

"Why does it keep asking for my password?"

Translation: *Please don't make me feel small.*

"Why do my emails disappear?"

Translation: *I don't trust this system.*

"My grandkids got me this, but I don't want to bother them."

Translation: *I want to learn without becoming a burden.*

So I answered with clarity, and I answered with reassurance. No shame. No tone. No "how do you not know this?" Just: "No worries. You're doing great. We can undo anything. This is not a test."

And you could watch shoulders drop. You could watch people get brave.

Because the moment someone swiped and the screen moved the way it was supposed to, they didn't just feel like they learned a gesture.

They felt like they could still learn.

And that's not tech. That's dignity.

After the class, people came up like it was a graduation ceremony. They wanted to shake my hand. Ask one more question. Tell me about their grandkids. And then—like a rhythm—they'd say, "Do you have a card?"

Business cards mattered then. A business card wasn't just contact info—it was proof you were real.

So I handed them out. And the sweetest older ladies took my card like it was a coupon for peace.

Within a week, my phone started ringing.

"Hi bud. You taught that class at the library."

That sentence became the start of a lot of good relationships.

At first, the calls were simple.

"Can you show me video calling?"

"Can you connect me to Wi-Fi?"

"Can you make my email show up again?"

Then the calls got more honest.

"Listen... my phone is acting weird."

Not weird in a scary way—weird in the modern way: it's doing things I didn't ask it to do.

And then the big question: "Can you show me how to use FaceTime?"

That question is not just technical. At that point, you enter a relationship.

That's when I learned something important: house calls weren't really about tech. They were about people.

People who have a need to be heard. To be validated. To be taught.

A lot of retirees don't want to drag their devices somewhere and sit in a waiting room feeling confused. They'd rather have someone kind come to them. Someone calm. Someone who can sit at the kitchen table like a nephew and say, "No worries—we'll get it."

And that became me.

I started seeing an invisible economy at work—an economy powered by kindness and trust.

People didn't recommend me because I was flashy. They recommended me because I was steady.

"He was so polite."

"He didn't make me feel dumb."

"He was honest."

That last one is the big one. Honesty travels. And dishonesty travels faster.

So I treated honesty like a moral duty and a business strategy.

If you want to understand modern human suffering, don't start with wars.

Start with passwords.

A sweet older lady will sit down and say, "It's asking me for a password."

And I'll say, "Okay—do you know it?"

And she'll say, "Yes."

Then she'll type something and it won't work.

"That's weird."

Then she'll type something else.

"That's weird."

At this point, "weird" is no longer a description. It's a coping mechanism.

Then she'll lean in like she's confessing: "I may have written it down somewhere."

And "somewhere" means: in a place that made sense at the time, but does not make sense now.

So we start searching. And "searching for a password" is not searching.

It's archaeology.

It's drawers full of rubber bands and mystery keys.

It's sticky notes from 2014 that say "Email: ???"

It's notebooks where passwords are written like riddles:

"Email — maybe?"

"Bank — old one?"

"New login — ask Susan."

Susan is not present. Susan has moved. Susan is now a legend.

And while we dig, the person keeps apologizing.

"I'm sorry, I'm such a mess."

And I always say the same thing: "You're not a mess. This is normal."

Because it is normal. Technology expects people to act like computers.

But humans are not computers.

Humans are emotions and memories and paper notes and "I thought I'd remember it."

So the work isn't just fixing the password.

The work is lowering shame.

Because shame makes people panic, and panic makes people forget everything.

So I kept it calm. I kept it kind. And eventually we found it—or we reset it—and they looked at me like I performed a miracle.

But I didn't perform a miracle.

I just stayed patient longer than the system did.

That's when you stop being "the tech guy" and become the family's on-call calm center. Sometimes, when your phone number is easily accessible, it is also easily dialed, maybe too easily at times. You know it is the case when you receive an accidental *video* call.

If you've never been accidentally video-called by senior to yourself, you haven't lived.

Like I said, being asked about FaceTime opens the door to your emotional support tech powers.

They don't know what they did. They don't even know they did it. So you answer the videocall and you're looking at a ceiling... or a forehead... or the inside of a purse.

Then you hear, "Hello? Hello? Is someone there?"

And you say, "Hi! I can see you."

And they say, "You can? Oh no!"

Then the screen shakes like the phone is being wrestled. Finally, you see their ear up close on your home screen and they whisper, "How do I get out of this?"

And you keep your voice gentle, because this is serious to them.

"Okay—press the red button."

"I don't see a red button."

And that's when you remember: when someone is nervous, their eyes stop working.

So you guide them calmly, step by step—until they press it and the call ends.

Then they call back normally, on purpose, to apologize.

"I'm so sorry."

And you say, "No worries at all."

Because it's honestly adorable. And it reminds you: humans don't come pre-installed with tech instincts. We learn.

People think tech support is about knowing devices. It is... but it's also not.

Most of my work was giving people their calm back.

Because when a phone "does something" to an older person, it doesn't feel like a small inconvenience. It can feel like the modern world is passing them by—like they're losing control.

So I learned to enter homes not as a "computer guy," but as a calm presence who knew the steps.

I wasn't just fixing a device.

I was helping a person feel capable again.

And there is no better feeling than seeing someone's face change when they realize, *Oh—I can do this.*

That's what built the business.

Not cleverness. Not hype. Not tricks.

Just steady service, plain speech, and protecting dignity.

Most people don't need a genius. They need support. Sometimes tech but always as a person. They need someone steady who can lower the shame and raise the confidence one small step at a time.

Super doesn’t require a cape.

CHAPTER 12

"Sweetheart" Means "You Saved My Video"

Florida taught me something I didn't fully understand growing up:

In some places, life runs on money.

In some places, life runs on status.

In Florida—especially inside organized retiree communities—life runs on reputation.

And reputation runs on calm.

It's not just what you can do. It's how you make people feel while you do it.

If my library classes were the quiet, educational version of entertainment for retirees, my buddy brought the full show. He started out as a construction worker—hard hat, dusty shirts, early mornings. The kind of guy who can carry half a house up a ladder and then casually eat a sandwich like it didn't count as exercise.

Then work got slow. Not because he was lazy. Just one of those seasons where the phone doesn't ring, and you start counting days like you're counting pennies.

His mom worked at a nursing home and knew two things at the same time: her son needed the money, and the residents needed joy. So she set him up to sing.

Not on a big stage. In a dining hall. With an audience that has seen everything.

A nursing home crowd is the most honest crowd on earth. They don't fake-laugh out of politeness. If they like you, you'll know. If they don't... you'll also know.

Sometimes someone falls asleep right in the middle of your best song—not because you're bad, but because it's 7:30 p.m. and their body is loyal to the schedule.

But if they do like you? It's beautiful.

Faces soften. People sing quietly. Someone taps a finger like they're remembering what dancing felt like. And you realize entertainment isn't shallow. It can be medicine.

That night, the residents went back to their rooms, gathered money, and handed him five hundred dollars.

Not a tip. Applause... paid in cash.

And it hit him the way it hits any person with a good heart: *I might be meant for this.*

Watching him swap a hard hat for a microphone did something to my brain. It reminded me that "what you do" isn't a life sentence—it's a season. And seasons change whether you're ready or not. Even if your routine fits like a round peg in a round hole, life still has a way of adding ruts, detours, and surprise potholes—just to keep you humble and paying attention.

He had to learn a whole new kind of discipline too. Appointments. Dates. Schedules. Practice. Rehearsal. It wasn't easy. It was work—just a different kind of work.

And none of it happened by accident. Somewhere behind the curtain was a person with a pen making sure joy showed up on time.

That world introduced me to a special kind of leader.

Not loud. Not flashy. Not speech-making.

Just steady.

Clipboard People.

The ones who quietly run everything with a pen, a sign-in sheet, and the calm confidence of someone who has seen every kind of human behavior and is no longer surprised by it.

And if you've never watched a Clipboard Person direct a room full of adults, you haven't seen real leadership.

Because retirees do not "have free time." They have scheduled time. Their calendar looks like an airport terminal:

Coffee.
Committee.
Lunch.
Nap.
Bridge.
Exercise.
Dinner.
Early bedtime.

And somewhere in there: the urgent need to learn what "the cloud" is.

So if you want to host a class or schedule a show, you don't compete with "nothing." You compete with everything.

A normal person says, "We start at six."

A Clipboard Person says, "We start at 6:02."

Not 6:00. Not 6:05. 6:02.

And once you've lived it, you understand: it isn't intensity. It's wisdom. Because at 6:00, people are still walking in. At 6:01, someone is still finishing a hallway conversation. At 6:02, everyone is seated, the door is closed, and peace has arrived.

So when my wife and I showed up on a Friday night to watch my buddy perform, I already knew who the real headliner was: the person with the clipboard and the clock.

The room was packed. Chairs full. Smiles wide. People dressed like they were going somewhere important—because to them, this was important.

My wife looked happy—quiet, content, the way she looks when life feels simple and safe.

And I remember thinking, Don't turn into the tech guy in public.

I tried to sit there like a normal husband. I smiled. I clapped. I pretended my hands didn't itch to troubleshoot anything within a ten-foot radius.

That thought lasted about three minutes.

A woman leaned in from behind us and whispered, "Hey bud... can you help me real quick?"

She held her phone out like an emergency flashlight. Not aggressive. Just trusting.

"I want to record him. But it keeps saying it can't."

I looked down and saw it immediately: Storage Almost Full.

There is a special sadness when a phone announces "Storage Almost Full" right when a person is trying to capture a memory. It doesn't feel like information. It feels like the phone saying, "Not now."

So I did what I've learned to do first.

I kept it calm.

"No worries, sis. We can fix this."

Running out of storage is the modern version of a closet door that won't shut. You didn't throw a party in there. You just lived. And life accumulates—photos, messages, apps, downloads you forgot, and that one video of your dog doing something completely normal... except emotionally it was precious.

When you check storage, the biggest category is almost always Photos.

Of course it is.

People don't take one picture. We take eleven pictures of the same thing, then keep all eleven, because deleting feels like admitting we were uncertain.

So I asked permission first, because trust matters.

"Do you mind if we delete a few duplicates?"

And I said it clearly: "We're deleting duplicates—not memories."

Her shoulders relaxed immediately. Duplicates are safe. Duplicates feel like cleaning.

Then we hit the part nobody expects: Recently Deleted.

Recently Deleted isn't trash. It's a 30-day "are you sure?" The phone is still holding your deleted stuff like a concerned friend.

That's when you go in and finally say, "Okay. Thank you. You can let it go now."

Back in the room, the camera opened like it wasn't mad anymore.

She hit record. The little red dot appeared.

Her eyes lit up. "Oh! It's working."

And she touched my arm and said, "Thank you, sweetheart."

In that community, that word doesn't mean romance. It means, "Thank you for helping me keep a memory."

Here's what makes this work strange: the simplest fixes often get the biggest relief.

A phone won't ring because a quiet moon icon is on.

A TV "won't work" because the input got changed.

One tiny setting can turn a peaceful home into a low-grade crisis.

And when you restore it, people don't thank you for being a genius. They thank you for being steady.

House calls taught me a different kind of truth too: almost every visit starts with hospitality.

"Do you want coffee?"

In Florida, that's not a question. That's a character test.

If you say no, you feel like you rejected their kindness. If you say yes, you have accepted a cup of love that comes with extra conversation.

And sometimes the technical fix takes five minutes... but the visit takes an hour.

Not because the person is wasting time. Because the person is lonely. Or kind. Or they finally have someone in the house who will listen without rushing.

If you're not careful, you treat that like an inconvenience.

If you're wise, you treat it like part of the job.

Because dignity can't be rushed.

And reputation travels fast in those communities—at the speed of a golf cart.

You help one person, and two more already know your name. Not because you advertised. Because someone said, "He was kind." "He explained it clearly." "He didn't make me feel dumb."

That's the whole business model right there.

And it's a good one.

My buddy adapted with a microphone. I adapted with a settings menu. Same lesson, different outfit: stay useful, stay kind, and be ready when life rearranges the room without asking permission.

Adaptability isn't becoming someone else; it's staying yourself while life changes the room.

Super doesn't require a cape.

CHAPTER 13

Before I Get Whacked

In the Midwest it's common to stay put—one town, one street, sometimes one house.

That's not a bad thing. It's steady, predictable, comfortable, familiar—everything you want in a family.

My father-in-law has lived on the same street for more than fifty years. In the same house.

He is a man of few words.

Not in a cold way. In a steady way.

He can communicate a full opinion with one "yep," and if you aren't paying attention, you'll miss how much he cares.

He's a retired tool-and-die man. Tool-and-die men don't guess. They measure. They solve. They make things fit the way they're supposed to fit. That kind of work shapes you. It makes you practical. It makes you allergic to nonsense. It gives you hands that can fix things without needing a speech afterward.

He knows everybody.

Not in an "I follow you online" way.

In a real way.

You drive down the street with him and he points like he's reading a living record.

"That's Bill."

"His dad worked over there."

"Good people."

And he says "good people" the way a man says a blessing.

Because to him, character matters. He doesn't talk about morals like a speech. He lives morals like a routine: show up, work hard, be honest, take care of family, help your neighbor. No drama. No slogans. Just consistency.

After my mother-in-law passed away, the family had to adjust. Grief changes the sound of a house. It leaves empty spaces where someone used to be.

In those seasons you learn what love is made of. Sometimes love is not emotional. Sometimes love is practical. A phone call. A meal. Showing up when it isn't convenient.

And my father-in-law might not say much, but he notices. If you do something kind, you'll get a simple "thank you." From him, that means more than a paragraph.

One time I fixed a small tech issue for him. Not heroic. Just a little thing. He watched quietly, nodded, and said, "You're pretty good at that."

To most people, that's a normal compliment. From him, that felt like a medal. Because when a tool-and-die man says you're "pretty good," what he's really saying is: I trust you.

I told my wife later that day, like a little kid who got praised by a coach, "Your dad said I'm pretty good at that."

She smiled. "That's a big deal."

And she was right.

He's not perfect. None of us are. But he's steady. And being around steady people teaches you things you can't learn from speeches.

But when you move to other places, you get to learn other colors of people—tones you've never heard, habits you didn't know existed, flavors that wake up your senses like fireworks on a cool fall evening. You discover how big the world is—and how unlimited your ability to grow can be.

If there's one thing every human wants—right up there near oxygen and coffee—it's this: to be accepted. Not famous. Not admired by strangers online. Accepted in the places that count: your family, your community, the room you're standing in right now.

Because being relatable isn't just a nice feature. Being relatable is survival. It's the difference between feeling like you belong... and feeling like you're visiting your own life.

I remember the first time I met an Australian. It was in Melbourne. We did the introductions, shook hands, and within about thirty seconds he said something like, "Hey... reckon we're both auzzies!"

Now my brain had to work fast, because an "auzzie" could be:

A guy from down under.

A heavy metal person.

A Midwestern fan of stories featuring tornadoes, little people, and a dog named Toto.

So I stood there smiling like I understood, thinking, "Okay... I'm not any of those things. But I am from the Midwest, and tornadoes are part of my cultural heritage."

And the fact that he started with humor—right away—made him instantly relatable.

There's a social skill in that: a joke that's just confusing enough to make you laugh before you fully understand it. It breaks the ice without breaking anyone.

I'll admit, my Midwest imagination had expected my first Australian to be... a character. Boots. Sun. Possibly a wrestling with a crocodile story. And maybe a shiny knife the size of a canoe paddle.

Instead, he was just a normal guy. Friendly. Funny. Relaxed.

And it was my first reminder that impressions are powerful—especially the ones you absorb young and never check.

That lesson hit me again when we moved to New Jersey, right outside Philadelphia.

First rule: you don't call it a "Philly cheesesteak" when you're near Philly. That's like walking into your kitchen and saying, "Ah yes, my home residence."

No. It's a cheesesteak.

Second rule: the beach is not "the beach." It's the shore.

And if you call it the beach in Jersey, nobody corrects you gently. They correct you with a look that says, "Oh, you're new-new."

The Jersey look is a cousin of the Midwest look—same power, less casserole.

Now let me tell you about the day my imagination nearly got me escorted out of a furniture store.

We drove fifty minutes to get to this furniture store. Fifty. The kind of drive where you start questioning every life decision that led you to needing a couch in the first place. But we did it. We pulled in like responsible adults with a mission.

Best part? We walk in a full hour before closing. The sign on the door says they close at five. It's four. We're early. We're punctual. We're practically model citizens.

The moment we step inside, a voice from the back area of the store yells, "We're closed!" It was dark. No faces. Just the voice.

Now, if you're from the Midwest, that's enough to make you apologize for the air you're breathing. But my wife—kind, sweet, and quietly unstoppable—smiles and says, "Oh! Well, the sign says you close at five, and it's only four."

The voice shoots back, "We're closed early."

My wife doesn't get rude. She doesn't get loud. She just gets politely persistent—the most dangerous form of determination. "Oh please," she says, still smiling. "We drove almost an hour to get here. I think I know what I want. Can we just see?"

Then someone blurts out, "Ay, Tony, I can take care of dem."

And that's when they appear.

Let's call them Vito and Bugsy. (Names changed.)

And just to be clear: in my head, they were Vito and Bugsy.

Vito comes out of the back like the manager of a place where rules are flexible and confidence is mandatory. Gold rings. Gold necklace. The kind of jewelry that makes you feel like he could sell you a couch or sell you a boat, depending on your tone.

He shakes my hand, which in turn shakes my whole body.

"Ay! I'm Vito. Dis is Bugsy. Don't mind Tony, he's not havin' a good day. Welcome in. Lemme guess—you're just lookin'?"

Bugsy is standing behind Vito. Quiet and pensive.

Now listen—if you grew up in the Midwest, your brain does not hear "Vito and Bugsy." Your brain hears theme music. Your brain hears a violin sting. Your brain goes, "This is the scene where a guy thinks he's buying a couch... but instead is asked to step into the back for no reason and ends up in a documentary".

So I'm fighting two realities at the same time:

Real reality: they sell furniture.

Midwest movie reality: I am about to become a cautionary tale.

We start walking through the showroom and there it is—the couch. The one with the little sign:

DISPLAY ONLY— PLEASE ASK ASSOCIATE.

Which is a polite way of saying: this couch is too expensive for the way you sit.

My wife—classy, calm, emotionally stable—treats the sign like a normal boundary. She says, "Sit down. Try it."

I treat the sign like a trap. Because in my imagination, the couch you're not supposed to sit on is exactly the couch that causes problems.

Vito points at it like it's harmless. "Go ahead. Sit. It's comfortable."

Bugsy smiles and adds, "C'mon. You're not marryin' it."

So I sit the way a Midwestern man sits when he's trying to survive: stiff, hands on knees, smiling too much—like I'm interviewing to be a couch owner.

Vito squints at a tag. "Lemme see if we got it in stock." Then he tells Bugsy, "Go in back and check if we got dis one, next to all dos bags on da floor".

And I don't know what it is about "the back" of a store, but "the back" always feels mysterious. The back is where truth lives. The back is where employees go to talk about you.

That is where you see the difference between a husband and a wife.

A husband's imagination will sprint into the woods with no map.

A wife will calmly remain in the living room and ask practical questions.

Bugsy comes from the "back" and gives a thumbs up.

Vito turns to us, friendly as can be, and says, "So... you like da couch?" He states, "Dat's da one, ya dink? Let's do dis deal. Bada-bing, bada-bam."

My brain goes: This is it. Say yes and you're in. Say no and you insult them. Either way—trouble.

So I stand up too fast. I bump a coffee table.

I whisper to my wife, "We need to leave... before I get whacked."

My wife doesn't blink. She smiles sweetly at Vito and says, "What other patterns does this pillow come in?"

Vito lights up. "Oh we got options. You want classy? You want cozy? You want 'my mother's gonna judge this'?"

My wife has nerves of steel. I'm over here living in a crime movie, and she's shopping for accent decor like she's in a catalog.

That's when I realized: they're just furniture salesmen. They're not involved in anything. They're trying to sell you a couch.

And I'm standing there having an internal crisis because I've realized how impressions work: they turn normal people into characters before you even meet them.

And that's not fair.

Impressions we have, many times can be far from the truth.

Because most people are just trying to live. Trying to be recognized. Trying to be accepted. Trying to sell you a recliner that won't ruin your back.

What people want isn't to be admired. It's to be seen correctly. Not as a stereotype. Not as a label. Not as a role. Just as a person.

Once you start noticing that, you realize how often we mis-see each other. We assume. We categorize. We project. And then we wonder why people feel lonely.

By the time you've lived a little—moved a few times, met people from different places, sat in rooms where you're the "new one"—you learn something:

Belonging is not the same as blending in.

Blending in is when you change yourself so nobody notices you're different.

Belonging is when you stay yourself, and people still make room for you.

When you walk into a new community, most of us get tugged toward one of two temptations: perform (be impressive, be funny, be liked), or withdraw (stay guarded, don't risk embarrassment).

I've done both. Sometimes I over-talk because I want the room to go well. Sometimes I under-talk because I don't want to be misunderstood.

True belonging happens when you relax into who you are—without putting on a show.

And the values that travel well are simple: honesty, kindness, respect, self-control, hospitality. You can bring those anywhere without being weird about it, because you're not forcing beliefs on people. You're just being decent.

Humor helps too—when it's kind. Humor can be a passport, as long as it doesn't embarrass people or punch down. When in doubt, make yourself the punchline. That style of humor is safe.

And safe people are rare in a loud world.

Different people aren't problems to solve—they're lessons to learn from, if you show up curious instead of suspicious.

Super doesn't require a cape.

CHAPTER 14

Belt Off, Dignity On

You can learn people in your own community. But if you want the full variety pack, don't go to a lecture.

Go to an airport.

An airport is a stress test for the human spirit, and it's also a comedy club if you're paying attention. Travel doesn't just show you the world. Travel shows you—you. It shows what you do when you're hungry, tired, and slightly confused while standing behind a man in sandals acting shocked that security wants him to remove them.

There's always a moment at TSA when a grown man discovers he's been wearing a belt his whole life and never realized belts have consequences.

The first time it happened to me, I stepped up confident. Shoes off. Laptop out. Liquids bag ready.

Then the agent looked at me like a calm judge and said one word: "Belt."

Now, friend, I didn't hear "belt" as an instruction. I heard "belt" like it was an indictment.

So I unbuckled it and tried to remove it smoothly, like I wasn't casually undressing in public. But belts don't come off smoothly. Belts come off like your asking them to surrender—tug, snag, and suddenly you're negotiating with your denim in public.

My wife, meanwhile, does TSA like she's trained. No drama. No extra items. No mysterious jingling. She'll look at me with a face that says, "Why are you always in an event?"

I'm not trying to be. I'm just built like a coat rack and TSA treats coat racks with suspicion.

Every airport has one holy place, and it's not the gate. It's the coffee stand.

I don't "like" coffee. I love coffee. I love it the way a person loves something that helps them stay kind. Coffee is how I re-enter the world without bumping into everybody.

My wife is gracious about this. She doesn't tease me. She'll just ask, "Do you want to grab coffee before we sit down?" And that is love. That's a woman noticing what keeps me calm and helping me get it before I become a problem.

Once I'm caffeinated, I can actually notice what she's been doing the whole time: finding calm on purpose.

My wife has this habit of finding quiet—and travel doesn't break it, it strengthens it. New signs, new rules, new rhythms... it's exciting, but it's loud. So we still look for calm. In our normal routine of life, looking for calm is sometimes an early morning walk when life is still waking up. Sometimes it's near a body of water at dusk. Or, as in an busy airport, sometimes it's just stepping away from the crowd and finding air.

What I love is she doesn't need a perfect moment to enjoy life. She can enjoy the small moment. A clean sidewalk. A cool breeze. A bench. A view. That's wisdom.

Every couple has the photo debate. One person wants to document everything. The other person wants to experience everything.

You'd think I'd be the photo person because I'm the tech guy—but I'm the "experience it first" person. My wife will quietly say, "Do you want a picture?" And she's not demanding it. She's offering future joy. Pictures aren't just for now—they're for later.

So we do the couple thing where we try to look normal and happy while also arguing softly about angles.

"Move left."

"The sun's in my eyes."

"You always squint."

"I'm not squinting. I'm being present."

Then we laugh and take the picture, and later we look at it and say, "That was a good trip."

Airport gate can test character though, especially the dreaded gate change. The screen flips. The announcement happens. The airport shuffle begins—that unique walk where people try to move fast while pretending, they aren't panicking.

My wife looks up, looks at me, and says, "Okay. Let's go."

No huffing. No blaming. No emotional speech. Just "okay."

She doesn't spend energy on what can't be changed. She saves it for what can be done. And I follow her calm like it's a map.

Getting on the plane is just as challenging.

Overhead bins turn normal people into athletes. A bin isn't just a bin—it's territory.

And because I'm tall, strangers assume I'm the unofficial overhead-bin employee.

"Can you help me with this?"

"For sure, friend."

Then I lift their bag and realize it weighs the same as a small appliance. Now I'm committed. I hoist it up, angle it, wrestle it into the bin while the bin fights back like it has a personality.

Finally it fits.

They say, "Oh thank you young man," and I smile like it was easy.

Then I sit down and whisper to my wife, "That bag was a piano."

She smiles and says, "You're sweet," which is her way of saying, "Please don't get injured for strangers."

Travel hands you a hundred tiny chances to practice being decent: how you treat tired workers, how you handle delays, how you talk to your spouse when you're hungry. The choices are small—but they add up fast.

My wife helps me with that, not by lecturing, but by modeling.

I need to confess something my wife already knows:

I try hard.

I really do.

I try to be thoughtful, prepared, responsible... all the good words.

But sometimes, even when you try hard, you still do something that makes your sweetie stare at you in silence like she's watching a documentary about life before checklists.

This is one of those chapters.

And because I'm me, I decided we weren't just going to travel—we were going to travel correctly. Passports, confirmations, chargers for chargers—the Olympics of paperwork.

So I found Global Entry.

Global Entry sounds like something superheroes have. Like you flash a badge and breeze through airports with a calm wind behind you.

We applied. Then we learned the part they don't put on the brochure: you have to sit with a government official who looks into your soul and decides whether you deserve shorter lines.

My wife went first and got the behemoth officer. Broad, refrigerator-shoulders type—intimidating from every angle.

Then I walked up to my window and saw a small skinny guy call my name, and I thought, "Oh good. This will be easy."

That confidence lasted six seconds.

Because small doesn't mean soft. Small sometimes means concentrated. Like espresso.

He evaluated my paperwork like it had personally disappointed him. Then the questions came rapid fire.

"Where are you going?"

"Why?"

"Where do you work?"

"Where were you born?"

"Your dad?"

"Your mom?"

"Do you have a dog?"

Now listen—"Do you have a dog?" is not a normal question in that lineup. It's like a chef asking, "And what is your relationship with parsley?"

It caught me off guard, and when I get caught off guard I start answering like a guilty man even when I'm innocent. Emotionally I shrank. Physically I can't. I'm tall. My body doesn't know how to look less suspicious.

Finally, Espresso Officer stared at me one last time and said, "Approved."

Approved. Like I had survived walking the plank.

I walked back to my wife trying to look calm. She smiled like she knew I had been through something.

I said, "I think that man can smell fear."

Going on international travel did get easier after that, though it doesn't absolve your need to be attentive to rules.

One time on our way home, heading to an international flight, we stopped at the airport breakfast stand. I grabbed an orange like a man trying to be healthy and responsible.

We were moving fast, staying on time—bags, lines, passports, shoes, belts—all checked. And my brain did what it does when there are ten tasks: it picked the fastest solution.

I saw an open spot in my wife's backpack and slipped the orange in there without thinking. Not maliciously. Not dramatically. Just... autopilot. I didn't smuggle it with criminal intent. I smuggled it with bad multitasking.

Later, after arriving back into the county, we were at Customs. My wife's bag gets stopped and opened. The officer pulls something out and asks, "What is this?"

My wife, genuinely confused, says, "I don't know how that got in my bag."

And she meant it.

But I knew. The memory hit me like a notification you can't dismiss: the orange.

The problem—I was already on the side of the glass door that reads DO NOT STOP, DO NOT ENTER.

My heart sank.

The officer continued asking my wife questions. Questions that should have been for me. But she took them and answered them honestly and calmly.

They are serious about fruit.

Not because they're mean. Because fruit can carry problems you don't want introduced into places that grow things for a living. Especially Florida. Florida doesn't play about citrus.

The officer gave her a controlled lecture—not yelling, but the kind of steady seriousness that makes you feel educated and judged at the same time.

Watching from the distance, the officer smirked and waved her through like nothing happened..

Which is airport for: *We remember you.*

She walked out holding her bag like it had betrayed her.

I was standing there on the "do not stop" side, trying to look like a supportive husband and not a man who just framed his wife with citrus.

My wife looked at me and said, quietly, "Did you put that in my bag?"

I said, "Yes, love."

She didn't shame me. She corrected me the way she does—gentle and devastating.

"Okay... please don't do that again."

I said, "I will never smuggle produce again."

And I meant it.

After that, we became convinced her name landed on one of those invisible lists. The kind you never get to read, but you feel it in the way people suddenly pay attention to your zippered compartments.

It felt like her passport had an invisible sticky note that said:

"Check her bag. Her husband is a produce man."

We became disciplined travelers though. No snacks. No "we'll eat it later." We started treating oranges like contraband.

And honestly, it probably made us better. Not because we got scared. Because we got humbled.

And lessons do not seem to happen in ones. They tend to happen until you get the point, sometimes multiple times.

Here's the thing about my wife: she's thoughtful. She gives gifts that say, "I want your life to feel better."

But airports are not designed for thoughtful gifts. Airports are designed for socks, chargers, and emotional damage. So anytime we try to bring something thoughtful, the airport acts like we've brought a riddle.

One time she brought her sister a candle—a real nice one. Wooden wick, cozy smell, the kind that makes you want coffee and forgiveness.

On a scanner, that candle did not look like comfort.

She got pulled aside. They opened the bag and stared at it like, "Explain yourself."

My wife stood there polite and wide-eyed like a librarian who accidentally walked into a SWAT briefing.

Then they realized it was a candle and everybody had to pretend they never suspected anything.

No apology. Just a professional reset: "Alright. You're good."

My wife nodded like she'd passed an exam she didn't study for.

Then there was the smoked salmon incident in Chile. She wanted to bring some back to her parents, because when you taste something that good you want the people you love to have a bite of joy without leaving their kitchen.

It was wrapped nicely, like a proper gift. To us, it was food. To security, it was a mysterious package that looked like it had been assembled by someone with confidence.

They held it up. "¿Qué es esto?"

My wife answered in English, because nerves send you home. "Smoked salmon."

"¿Qué?"

Volume became their translator.

So my wife tried the shorter word: "Salmon."

Under pressure, it apparently sounded like a word you do not want to accidentally say in an airport. I watched the officers posture shift. Not a panic. Not drama. Just that serious movement that says, "We are not playing".

So I'm standing there thinking, Lord, please help my wife pronounce a fish.

She slowed down like she was spelling her name at the pharmacy.

"S... A... L... M... O... N."

One of them nodded. "Ah."

Category restored. The universe calmed down.

Somewhere between the belts, the background checks, and the salmon spelling bee, I learned something: my wife and I weren't just traveling.

We were practicing patience—together—one awkward checkpoint at a time.

Airports have a way of reminding you you're not in charge... even when you packed the bag yourself.

So yes, we visited places, but mostly we saw people, the real flavors of life.

In unfamiliar places, humility is the best passport.

Super doesn't require a cape.

CHAPTER 15
Perdón While I Panic

Before you picture me as rugged, let's get one thing straight: I'm not.

I am not a cowboy.

I am not a rugged outdoorsman.

I'm the kind of man who can set up a Wi-Fi network, troubleshoot a printer, and explain why your phone storage is full. But put me on top of a living animal with opinions, and suddenly my confidence becomes... theoretical.

Still, Chile has a way of convincing you that you're capable of more than you are. Or maybe it just convinces you to try things you're underqualified for. Either way, my wife and I were there with longtime friends, and we signed up for one of those horseback rides that looks like a calm scenic stroll in the brochure.

You know the kind.

Four smiling people. One gentle trail. A guide who looks like he was born on a saddle. And horses standing there peacefully like they've never had a bad day in their lives.

The brochure forgets to mention the horses are sentient. They are not props. They are not amusement park rides. They are animals with personalities, instincts, and an alarming awareness of whether the person on their back has any business being up there.

Our guide introduced himself as Antonio. He had that calm competence that makes you feel safe and also slightly ashamed of your own life choices. He started matching everyone with horses.

He gave my wife a good-sized horse. He gave my buddy and his wife horses that looked strong but manageable.

Then he looked at me. Paused for half a second. And brought me a bigger horse.

Not a "tourist horse."

A mountain horse.

The kind of horse that doesn't just carry you—he evaluates you.

His name was Salvador.

Salvador was beautiful—dirty white and tan, solid, strong. But he also had an energy that didn't feel like cute excitement. It felt like he'd already written the schedule and I was simply invited to participate.

We set off through the mountains near Puerto Montt. The air was cool. Everything smelled green and alive—like your lungs were getting upgraded. The trail was muddy enough to make you question your footwear choices in life.

The horses didn't care. They moved through it like tanks. At times I could feel my boots dragging because the mud was reaching for them like it wanted to keep them.

Then Antonio did something that woke up my inner Midwest boy.

He reached into his saddle, pulled out a machete, and turned sharp left.

Not a subtle turn. A "new plan" turn.

He started clearing brush like it was a normal Tuesday. It was like watching someone pull out a sword in a grocery store and calmly open a new aisle.

My buddy's eyes got big.

His wife made a sound that was half delight, half concern.

My wife stayed calm, because that's what she does.

I watched the machete swing back and forth and thought, shortcut… or

helicopter?

Antonio carved a path and we climbed up what looked like an uncharted trail. Eventually we reached a clearing and approached a field fenced off with a gate. Antonio opened the gate while still on his horse—no drama, no hesitation—then motioned us through like he'd done it a thousand times.

I was right behind him.

As Salvador stepped into that open field, I felt him change. Subtle at first—like the shift you feel when a dog sees a squirrel. His body tightened. His head lifted. His ears angled forward.

It was like he look at the open space and said, "finally!"

And I'll admit it: deep down, part of me wanted speed. I didn't ask for it. I didn't say it out loud. But the desire was there—the way a teenage boy looks at a muscle car and thinks, this seems reasonable.

Salvador felt it.

I didn't cue him. He just decided we were doing this.

He took off.

Not a trot.

Not a jog.

He launched.

Zero to fast in about two seconds.

For a few seconds, it was glorious. Wind. Power. Full stride. The kind of moment where your imagination shows up early and tells you you're doing great.

Then reality arrived—politely, but firmly.

Because Salvador wasn't asking my permission.

He saw me up there and thought, Finally. Someone who can't file a complaint in Spanish.

Antonio reacted immediately. His horse was smaller than Salvador, but quick. He came after us like a man whose job depends on keeping tourists alive.

We had a big jump on him, and I learned a new truth in real time:

I was not controlling the ride.

Salvador was.

I pulled the reins to circle back toward the group. Salvador did turn, and for a brief moment I thought, Okay. Great. I'm in charge.

In my imagination, I did that gracefully—strong, skilled, majestic.

In reality, I'm sure I looked like a wet towel flapping on a clothesline in a windstorm.

We circled back toward the group, and instead of slowing down and rejoining like a polite horse, Salvador started circling them.

Fast.

We did multiple laps like it was a track meet nobody signed up for.

Antonio crossed near me, reaching like he might grab the reins. He was yelling Spanish—fast Spanish, urgent Spanish—and I couldn't understand him.

Since I couldn't understand, I chose to assume it was encouraging. That's how you stay calm as a tourist.

Our two friends were clustered together watching the scene like an audience that did not buy tickets. My buddy yelled something helpful that made no sense, like, "Jump!"

His wife was gasping, eyes wide open and fixed on seeing the ending.

And then I looked at my wife.

She was not watching.

Not because she didn't care—because she is wise.

Her horse had calmly taken the opportunity to eat fresh grass, and she was looking down and stroking its mane like she didn't want it to get any ideas.

In reality, she didn't want to see the ending.

That's marriage in one picture:

One spouse participating in chaos.

The other spouse preventing chaos from spreading.

I thought about jumping off. We were moving so fast. The field wasn't perfectly smooth. I imagined landing wrong, spending the next six months learning humility in traction.

Then I looked ahead.

A fence.

Tall—about six feet.

And Salvador was aimed at it like a man with confidence and no committee.

He was not slowing down.

He was not reconsidering.

He looked committed.

And my brain went, Oh. We're about to become a story.

Fifty feet.

Forty.

Thirty.

I braced for what felt like a heroic leap into the air and a disappearance into the Chilean wilderness.

Then Salvador stopped.

He stopped on a dime—less than ten inches from that fence.

It was the most sudden stop I have ever experienced on anything with legs.

My body did not stop.

I pitched forward and wrapped my long, lanky arms around Salvador's neck like a man hugging a tree in a tornado.

And here's the miracle:

He didn't throw me.

I stayed on.

Victory.

Well—victory until Antonio arrived.

Antonio caught up and did not ease into the moment. There was no gentle, "Hey bud, let's maybe not do that again."

There was Spanish. Fast Spanish. Loud Spanish.

The kind of Spanish that doesn't need translation because the volume is doing most of the work.

Antonio's tone said, "We are past polite."

Meanwhile, I was still wrapped around Salvador's neck—not to be dramatic, but to remain on Earth.

Antonio took the reins with one hand like he'd been doing it since birth and said something to Salvador that sounded like a command and a warning at the same time.

Salvador flicked an ear back like, "Oh. Him."

Then Salvador did what no horse has ever done in the history of horses.

He acted innocent.

He stood there breathing calmly, eyes wide, as if he had been quietly reflecting on nature the whole time.

I tried to help with the only Spanish I was confident in.

"Sí."

Now, "sí" is a useful word, but it's also dangerous.

Because it can mean "yes," and it can also mean, "I do not understand anything you just said, but I would like this moment to end."

In my case, it was both.

Antonio looked at me like he was deciding whether to scold the horse, scold me, or scold whoever raised me.

I attempted the next sentence—the one that always sounds correct in your head until it exits your mouth.

"Perdón... más despacio, por favor."

I said it with confidence and questionable pronunciation. It probably sounded like I was ordering a pastry.

Antonio replied—still fast, still intense, still in Spanish.

I nodded like a man who absolutely understood the safety briefing.

And that's when I realized something important about myself:

I was 25% fluent and 80% confident—dangerous on horseback.

I didn't catch all the words, but I caught the message: this isn't my workplace, and I'm not the boss of anything with hooves.

Antonio didn't negotiate. He pointed us back toward the trail and escorted me into formation like a schoolteacher walking the loud kid back to his desk.

My buddy's eyes were still big.

His wife was staring at me like she'd just watched someone try to juggle knives and then decide to do it on a trampoline.

The funny part is, I think they were trying to decide whether to laugh or pray.

My wife finally looked up. She looked at me, then at Salvador, then at Antonio—and she did the kindest thing a wife can do in a moment like that.

She didn't scold.

She didn't panic.

She just asked, calmly, "Are you okay?"

And I said, with the dignity of a man who had just survived by hugging a horse, "Yep."

One word. Midwest. Strong.

Salvador snorted like he was also saying, "Yep."

We finished the ride without further incidents, which is another way of saying I behaved like a man who had been warned by nature and respected the warning.

Antonio rode in front and kept glancing back—not angry glances, professional glances. The kind that say, I will finish this ride, but I am watching you.

And if you've ever been watched by a competent person after you did something dumb, you know the feeling.

It's humbling.

It's also good for you.

Because it reminds you: you are not the main character in someone else's workplace.

You are the risk they have to manage. That's the kind of humility that follows you out the door and across a border.

As we continued on, Chile didn't just humble us. Chile fed us.

And it didn't feed us the way a place feeds you when it wants your money. It fed us the way a place feeds you when it wants you to remember it.

We spent time along the coast—Valparaíso, Viña del Mar, and Puerto Montt—and coastal towns carry themselves with a kind of quiet confidence.

In the Midwest, if someone catches a fish, you'll hear about it for a week.

In Chile, the fish are just... there.

The boats are there.

The work is there.

The beauty is there.

Like it has nothing to prove.

One day we ended up in a small fishing village with a market that looked like a painting. Bright boats—reds, blues, yellows, greens—like the whole place had decided beige was not invited.

And here's what surprised me: there were fish everywhere, but it didn't smell fishy. It smelled like ocean air and work and cooking—clean, alive, not stale.

We found a row of tiny café rooms—one-room restaurants, really—run by fishermen's wives. Each room had one table that could seat maybe eight people if everyone liked each other.

No trendy décor. No concept. Just personal warmth and the quiet confidence of someone who knows how to feed people.

She handed us a menu.

Four items.

That's it.

Some people get nervous when there aren't enough choices. They feel like they might pick wrong.

I felt immediate peace.

Because I've been to restaurants where the menu is so big it feels like reading a binder. By the time you finish, your coffee is cold and you've aged emotionally. Then the waiter asks, "Any questions?"

"Yes. Mostly, why is the entire planet on this menu?'

But this little café room felt like being invited to her personal table.

We ordered simply. She went right into motion. Outside, you could see pots going, steam rising, shellfish and mussels and crustaceans thrown in like the sea itself was cooperating.

Then she served us Chilean sea bass.

I'm going to say it plainly:

It was the freshest sea bass I have ever eaten.

It tasted like butter that had been pulled straight out of the ocean.

Not "buttery."

Butter.

My wife took a bite and gave that quiet look that says, this is special, without needing to announce it.

My friend nodded like a man who wanted to say something wise but knew the correct move was to keep chewing.

I asked the woman how fresh it was. She answered in Spanish, and even with my limited understanding, I caught the part that mattered.

Her husband had gone out at three in the morning.

That fish was so fresh it still had the schedule of the man who caught it.

And right then I thought: we spend a lot of our lives paying for "quality," but sometimes the best quality isn't expensive because it's fancy.

It's valuable because it's honest.

As we ate, I kept looking out at those colorful boats tied to the shore, quiet and steady.

And a memory surfaced that I didn't expect.

After my aunt died, we found a Whistler etching in her attic—tucked away like someone had hidden a piece of history among boxes and dust. We had it restored. It was Whistler's

Fisherman's Wharf, sketched around the Thames in the late 1850s. Dramatic. Simple. Human.

We could have auctioned it, but the story felt worth more than the money.

It still hangs in my living room.

And sitting there in that Chilean village, looking at boats on the water, I felt that same quiet all over again—like the world was reminding me that beauty repeats itself.

Different countries. Different languages. Same dignity in work.

We continued on with our travels and after leaving the coast, somebody said the words "whitewater rafting," and I realized Chile wasn't done teaching me who I really was.

Apparently, my vacation itinerary was organized by someone who believes growth requires mild terror.

If you've ever been whitewater rafting, you've had an honest conversation with yourself.

A river does not care about your résumé.

It does not care about your plans for later.

It does not care that you watched one video and now feel "pretty confident."

A river will show you your courage, your panic, your pride, and your prayer life—all in about twelve seconds.

Our guide started the safety talk.

I'm a man who likes instructions. I like the idea that there is a correct way to do things.

But something happens when you put on a helmet and a life vest.

Your brain hears the words.

Your imagination adds pictures.

"If I fall out... don't panic... float feet-first... grab the rope..."

And your brain is like, Great. Excellent.

And your heart is like, we have made a terrible mistake.

My wife looked calm. She always looks calm.

And me? I was trying to look confident while quietly negotiating with God.

Not dramatic. Just respectful.

"Lord, thank you for this beautiful earth. Thank you for this river. I do not need to conquer it. I just need to survive it with dignity."

The guide demonstrated paddling.

Our guide was from Germany—spoke English, but with the kind of German accent that makes every sentence sound like a rule that already existed before you were born. And honestly? It helped. Because when a man like that gives a command, you don't consider it—you comply.

Within two minutes we weren't tourists anymore. We were a troop. A wet, nervous troop with helmets.

And our job was simple: listen intently... and obey immediately.

"Forward."

"Back."

"Stop."

"High side."

Now, "high side" is a phrase you don't appreciate until you need it.

Because "high side" means the raft is tilting and everyone needs to move their weight fast so it doesn't flip.

In other words: the raft is trying to become a memory, and everyone has to agree—quickly—that today is not the day.

When we pushed off, the river was calm at first.

That's always how it starts.

The river gives you a minute to get comfortable so your pride can stand up.

Then the rapid comes and the river knocks your pride back down like it owes the river money.

We hit the first real rapid and the raft started bouncing. Water came over the sides—not a polite sprinkle.

A full "welcome to the program" splash.

And something happened that I love about experiences like this:

We became a team.

No one cared who looked cool.

No one cared who had the best gear.

No one cared who was "good at this."

We just listened, paddled, leaned, held on, laughed, and survived.

And that teamwork wasn't theoretical.

There were eight of us in that raft, and the truth is: you don't go rafting as individuals. You go as a moving pile of humans who are all responsible for each other's bones. If one person goes out, everybody's job changes instantly.

That's exactly what happened.

We hit a big wave and the woman stationed right behind my wife got launched like Tinkerbell—just gone—right out of the boat.

Immediately the guide barked a command—short, sharp, no room for opinions—and my wife didn't hesitate. My girl went into action, reached down into that cold, churning water, grabbed that life vest like it owed her money, and hauled that woman back into the raft and into safety.

I'm not exaggerating when I say I felt like I was watching a heavyweight wrestler do a rescue in hiking shoes.

And the wild part is, my wife didn't celebrate. No speech. No "did you see that?"

She just reset her grip, checked the woman's face, and got right back into position like, "Okay. Paddle."

And in the middle of all that, I realized why people love rafting.

Not because it's dangerous.

Because it's alive.

It pulls you out of your head and puts you in the present.

And once you accept you're not the boss of the river, you can finally enjoy the ride.

By the time we got off the water, we were soaked, hungry, and quietly grateful—the kind of gratitude you feel when you've been humbled in a way that doesn't shame you, just straightens you out.

Chile did that.

With a horse.

With a meal.

With a river.

And with the steady kindness of people who were simply doing what they do well.

By the end of Chile, I realized you don't have to share a language to share a lesson. Urgency sounds the same in any tongue, competence looks the same in any uniform, and kindness feels the same at any table. I came in thinking travel was about seeing new places. I left remembering it's mostly about learning your place—on the horse, in the raft, and in other people's routines.

You can be brave without being loud: respect the risk, trust the guide, and stay teachable.

Super doesn't require a cape.

CHAPTER 16
The Teacher's Table

I'm not a teacher... except I keep ending up teaching anyway.

I've never had "Teacher" on a badge.

No degree. No formal title. No classroom keys dangling from my belt like a middle-school janitor who knows everybody's business.

But I've done what teachers do.

I've helped people understand things. I've walked someone through a hard day. I've shown somebody how to fix something, cook something, use something, apologize for something... and—more than once—how to avoid hitting "Reply All" like it's a self-defense button.

If you've ever helped someone get it, you've been a teacher for a minute.

And most of the time, teaching doesn't happen under fluorescent lights. It happens at the kitchen table. On a front porch. In a car ride. Over a workbench. In the hallway when someone stops you and says, "Hey... can I ask you something?"

That's the quiet superpower of a decent life: you learn—and then you pass on what you learned.

That's probably why AI grabbed my attention the way it did.

I'm fascinated by it—partly impressed, partly suspicious, like a shortcut that feels illegal even when it works. It's fast. It's useful. Sometimes it answers like a genius. Other times it answers like it's never met a human and doesn't want to start now.

I've pushed it. Tested it. Tried different models. Asked for insight. And after the first wave of "wow," I noticed something: it can start to feel... similar.

Sometimes it's like a blender—clear ingredients going in, mystery smoothie coming out. It can combine and summarize and remix. But it can't do the one thing that makes human teaching different: it can't hand you a lesson that cost it something.

Perspective has to be earned—and earning it takes time, bruises, and a few awkward apologies.

Humans learn through effort and failure. Through love and loyalty. Through choosing the right thing when it would be easier not to. Through being corrected and not turning into a courtroom about it. Over time, that becomes character. And character becomes the kind of wisdom you can give away without sounding like you're giving a speech.

AI is a tool—and it's a strong one.

But it doesn't have a life story behind its advice.

You do.

And once I started thinking that way, I realized I'd watched that lesson happen in real time—on a day that had nothing to do with computers.

We once hosted a kids day—parents and kids together—to give them a real taste of practical work. Not the "watch a video" version. The hands-on version.

And what surprised me wasn't how fast they picked things up—it was how hungry they were to feel capable.

A kid holds a tool correctly for the first time and stands a little taller.

A teen realizes, "Wait... I can actually learn this," and something in his face changes.

A parent watches it happen and gets quiet, because they can see confidence forming in real time.

Adults forget how powerful that feeling is—because we're busy paying bills, hunting keys, and wondering why the scissors keep relocating like they're on a mission. Kids don't forget.

You show them how something works, and you can see it in their eyes.

That spark.

That's why teaching matters.

And that day didn't just feel good. It taught me what being "a teacher" actually looks like—whether you're teaching a child, a friend, an apprentice, or just a person who's trying.

First: care about the learner.

People don't learn well when they feel small. They learn when they feel safe. Not coddled—safe. Safe to ask. Safe to try. Safe to be wrong without getting embarrassed for sport. If you care about the person, the lesson lands softer—and deeper.

Second: keep your tools clean—and stay flexible.

Your "tools" aren't just what's in your hand. They're your approach. Your patience. Your ability to explain the basics without acting annoyed that someone doesn't already know them. And the trap is trying to force every learner into one style.

If you really care, you adapt. You explain the what, where, when, how, and why—then you watch them take the fundamentals and blend them with their own gifts.

Because the goal isn't to create a copy of you.

The goal is to help them become a better version of themselves—steadier, smarter, more confident, more useful.

Third: stay out of the spotlight.

Have you ever been to a kid's play and watched a parent step onto the stage like, "Move over, honey. Let me show you how it's done."

That is pain.

That is secondhand pain.

Teaching isn't performing. Teaching is building.

When you're young, you're in the spotlight because you're learning. As you mature, the focus shifts. The joy becomes the fruit—what others are becoming because you helped them.

And if you keep your ego out of it, you'll stay satisfied.

Because growth is joy.

Now... none of this is new. I just didn't always have words for it.

My mom was doing it before I could spell it.

Throughout our childhood, during the summer she taught us to work, to can, to preserve—peaches, pickles, tomatoes, berries—so the fruit would still be there when the land wasn't giving anything back.

And then in winter—when everything outside looked dead and gray—she'd take a jar down, open it up, and the smell would hit you like a memory with a heartbeat. Still fresh. Like it had been harvested yesterday.

And we'd enjoy the fruit of summer labor long after the season had passed—even if we didn't personally do the work.

That's how good memories work too.

You live them. You keep them. And at the right time—when someone needs warmth, guidance, courage, or hope—you open the jar and share what helped you.

And when you share those memories—especially with the young ones, the ones who weren't there when it happened—they get to taste it too. They smell the aroma. They feel the scene. They live it with you.

And then, without you even realizing it, you've done something bigger than storytelling.

You've trained the next generation. You've become a teacher of teachers.

Not in a classroom. Not for a title. Not in a performance.

From a moment in your life.

A memory.

A person saying, "Here—this helped me. Maybe it'll help you."

If this whole book leaves you with one thing, let it be this: your small moments count. Your kindness counts. Your clean humor counts. Your steady love matters. Your willingness to keep learning matters.

And when you pass on what you've learned—quietly, humbly, patiently—you finish the story the right way.

Not with fireworks.

But with fruit in winter.

With a table that feels safe.

With a life that helped other lives grow.

Looking back, the pattern is obvious: I kept getting handed little tables. A kitchen table. A library table. A workbench. A seat beside someone who was nervous and needed calm more than answers. And somewhere between new technology, old wisdom, and a jar of peaches in January, I learned what teaching really is: you don't impress people into growth—you invite them into it. You make life feel less scary, one steady moment at a time.

The best teaching isn't loud—it's lived. And the most valuable lessons are the ones you pass on with patience and clean love.

Super doesn't require a cape.

Don't miss out!

Visit the website below and you can sign up to receive emails whenever James Alexander publishes a new book. There's no charge and no obligation.

https://books2read.com/r/B-A-JLEFF-AKJZI

BOOKS 2 READ

Connecting independent readers to independent writers.

www.ingramcontent.com/pod-product-compliance
Lightning Source LLC
LaVergne TN
LVHW052028080426
835513LV00018B/2221
* 9 7 9 8 2 1 8 9 3 0 6 7 7 *